Praise for the first edition

'This is a book for practitioners by practitioners. It offers must-read insights into the potential of data to transform. Whether de-mystifying the subject for busy C-Suite leaders, or offering practical checklists for first-time CDOs to benchmark progress, there's something here for anyone who cares about harnessing data to improve outcomes. Read. Smile. Exploit.'

Tim Carmichael, *Chief Data Officer and Chief Analytics Officer, British Army*

'Brilliant overview for CDOs and senior leadership teams on this emerging and disruptive role. It also offers the reader an understanding of how the CDO – as a catalyst – has the dual task of creating transformational value from data and to greatly contribute towards the new data-driven DNA of the organisation's vision of the future.'

Matt Corey, *MD, Change Force*

'*Nothing, literally nothing, works in a company without the input of data in some shape or form* . . . well said Caroline and Peter! *Data is indeed here to stay. We've got pundits exclaiming that, data is the new oil, the new currency, the new bacon* . . . To all Chief Data Officers and companies looking for a Chief Data Officer, this book is all you need to get started. Caroline and Peter have thought of everything including the first 100 days in the CDO office!'

Vanessa Eriksson, *Chief Data Officer Advisor, PwC*

'Without any doubt, this playbook is a must read for the primary audience, the CDOs. In my opinion, it is equally a must read for the secondary audience, the C-Suite, for the insight on how the role complements their businesses.'

Sham Kashikar, *ex-Chief Data Officer, Sales & Marketing, Intel*

'*The Chief Data Officer's Playbook* is the best overall resource available for CDOs and their teams. The release of this book is perfectly timed. The CDO Club tracks CDO hires globally, and last year alone the number of new CDO hires quintupled. The *Playbook* is a compendium of essential knowledge anyone operating in the current data environment must have.'

David Mathison, *Chairman, CEO and Founder, CDO Club/CDO Summit*

'In today's information-rich world, data-driven organisations have the competitive edge. Data analytics and data-driven insight make the difference between guesswork and timely, evidence-based decision making. Understanding the role of the Chief Data Officer (CDO) is the key to unlocking this potential. This handy, practical book gives you access to the expertise of market-leading practitioners who have harnessed the power of data to deliver real business gains in large-scale companies and organisations. Whether you are an executive looking to transform the use of data in your organisation or an aspiring CDO looking for hints and tips on how to develop your career and make a real impact, this is the book for you.'

Nick Poole, *Chief Executive Officer, CILIP*

'This practical guide is a must-read for data leaders building the foundation of value creation from data.'

Katia Walsh, *Chief Global Strategy and Artificial Intelligence Officer, Levi Strauss & Company*

The
Chief Data Officer's
Playbook

Second edition

The
Chief Data Officer's Playbook

Second edition

Caroline Carruthers and Peter Jackson

facet
publishing

Published by Facet Publishing
c/o British Library, 96 Euston Road, London NW1 2DB
www.facetpublishing.co.uk

Facet Publishing is wholly owned by CILIP: the Library and Information Association.

British Library Cataloguing in Publication Data
A catalogue record for this book is available from the British Library.

ISBN 978-1-78330-474-5 (paperback)
ISBN 978-1-78330-475-2 (ePDF)
ISBN 978-1-78330-476-9 (ePUB)

First published 2018
This second edition 2021

Typeset from authors' files in 11/14pt Myriad Pro and University Old Style by Flagholme Publishing Services.
Printed and made in Great Britain by CPI Group (UK) Ltd, Croydon, CR0 4YY.

Contents

List of figures

Preface

We started the preface of the first edition of this book with a short anecdote to set the scene; since then, much has changed. The ecosystem of the CDO has evolved, there are more CDOs and more organisations are trying to get their data under control and to leverage its value. However, that initial anecdote still is very relevant, so here goes.

We were on a panel at a conference discussing how to harness value from data – we've changed the discussion topic slightly so as to not identify the conference, event or other participants; to protect the 'not-so-innocent'. This topic, or a closely related one, has been a regular feature of the panels and discussions we've been involved with. It seems everyone is trying to get to the heart of that question and find the answer. Data has been seen as such an inconsequential thing, that just seemed to be there, in the past; but there is a growing respect for data as a really fundamental asset – which is a great thing.

Everyone knows, because we've all been told many times recently, that data is the new oil, or perhaps the new soil, the new sun, the new water, we've even heard a comparison to bacon. The question that then leads out of this is the one we have been facing: if data is the new oil, how does an organisation get value out of it? It is all very well having struck oil, but if you don't know how to get it out of the ground, or how to refine it into useful products, or that it can be transformed and manufactured into valuable products or consumed to create energy - what use is the oil in the ground? To be frank we really hate data is the new oil, because data is data and the analogy only goes so far before it falls really short on highlighting the power of data.

On that panel we began by responding to some prepared questions. There were some great and experienced minds on the panel: leaders in their respective fields and all practitioners from the hard edge of industry, business and commerce. We each took turns to discuss the great value that could be derived from data. We each provided stunning examples of what could be done with data to transform, disrupt and innovate organisations and industries. It is interesting to note that the topic was definitely worded as 'digital assets' but we all spoke about 'data', and used the term data and not digital asset. After 30 minutes the Chair opened the discussion to questions from the floor, and there it was, the question that has been asked, in our experience, over and over again, and this is it, nearly word for word:

> Thank you for the excellent discussion and the inspiring examples, but I would like to know how my organisation gets from where we are now to be in a position to exploit the opportunities in our data; to extract the sort of value which you have all been talking about.

Here is the pattern of responses that get handed down from the panels in response to that question: 'What you need is master data management', 'You need to bring all your data into a data lake/warehouse', 'You need to be able to ask the right question of your data', 'You need to establish true data ownership within the business'. On many occasions the audience either are happy with the responses, or aren't happy with the responses but don't want to show their ignorance and push for the sort of answer that they want. Either way, the outcome is pretty much the same, and that is where the discussion ends. But not on this occasion: the questioner listened patiently to the answers from this impressive panel and came back with his follow-up:

> Thank you again for your insight and suggestions. But how do you do those things? How does my organisation, and I am sure many others in this room, get from where we are today to be able to do the things you have just suggested so that we can then derive the fantastic value from our data like the examples you presented earlier? And I have written them all down to read up on later because they were like a foreign language to me.

Many of the conference-goers who attend these sessions focusing on deriving value from data are 'from the business'; they tend not to be 'data' professionals. They are CEOs, COOs or perhaps CFOs who want to understand how value can be derived from their data and, if data is the new oil, how do you unleash the energy within it?

Our answer to that question is 'Get yourself a Chief Data Officer as quickly as you can'. The Chief Data Officer (CDO) is the person who will take your organisation on the journey from where you are now to where you want to be. The CDO won't do this alone, the whole organisation will need to be part of making that journey possible, but the CDO will be the enabler, the one with the vision, the strategy, the technical specialism and the experience to guide the way. The first step for any organisation wishing to make that journey is getting to that realisation and then making the decision to recruit a CDO, and then to embrace and empower that person ... and be ready for changes.

In the past few years many organisations have got to this point, and there will be many more reaching this point over the next three years. Perhaps even the astute questioner's organisation reached that point and recruited a CDO shortly after that conference. Throughout the book we use the title CDO, but we realise that organisations do assign different titles for the person/role that effectively has the function of the CDO within their organisation. We are meaning the senior data leader within the organisation, whatever title you choose to use. This book is written for all of them and is meant to be inclusive for all in the senior data community.

The past two years

We have attended even more conferences and spoken at a lot more of them over the past two years. Many have been topic-specific, like the one just discussed: harnessing value from data, the power of big data, the opportunities of advanced analytics, machine learning, artificial intelligence (AI), master data management, among many more very specific data topics. Others have been aimed much more at data strategy and the function of this new, emerging CDO role. We have also founded the Chief Data Officer Summer School, which, as we write this new preface, is going into its third year and will have over 800 alumni across the world.

We had three motivations to write this book, and they hold true for this second edition. The first was that lots of people were asking questions about the role: What does it do? Where does it sit in the organisation? Where do you recruit one? How do you recruit one? Who does it report to and how do you become one? The second was that no one seemed to have the answers: there was a lot of great discussion but no clear set of instructions. The role was so new, emerging rapidly and evolving as it emerged. Finally, the current population of CDOs is quite small; the network is tight and interacts extremely well. We have found that this small, emerging group of professionals are very open to helping each other, discussing their experiences, sharing best practice, sharing their disasters and dilemmas. The network of CDOs is incredibly mutually supportive and eager to create a sustainable professionalism about what we do. Perhaps it is a case of pioneers sticking together.

These motivations came together for us at a data conference in London in November 2016. The enabler was meeting each other at this conference and agreeing that people who are taking up this role of CDO might benefit from having some sort of handbook or manual. That was the genesis of this book and we sincerely hope that it does help the growing community of CDOs and future CDOs. This second edition has been prompted by the gathering pace and evolution of the role and we wished to bring the content up to date with our growing experiences and conversations with the community of CDOs.

Originally the word 'playbook' was a sporting term used to denote various strategies for a team that, when used, tended to result in a win for the team. That is what we have created for you – various strategies, tools and results of our real-life experiences which can help you leapfrog some of the mistakes we have made and learn from where it went well for us. It is meant to be useful to you whenever you need some ideas about the next steps, whether that next step is the new role you are looking to try for, or if you are already a CDO and just need a reference guide to help you in the areas you might not have focused on in the past. It is deliberately simple and easy to read so that you can read the whole thing, or jump to the areas that you will get the most from.

When writing this book we had in our minds, and hearts, the present and future community of CDOs, so when we refer to 'you', we do mean 'you' the CDO. We have written the book in this style to personally address our friends and colleagues. Sometimes it has seemed more appropriate to refer to the CDO in the third person, but the CDO remains our primary audience.

However, though this book may be primarily written for present and future fellow CDOs, we do recognise that there is a secondary audience to address, and that is the rest of the C-Suite. We have tried to address this audience to help them understand the value that a CDO can bring to an organisation, what they do, how to recruit one, where they should sit within the organisation and whom they should report to. This is a playbook for the CDO and their colleagues, full of real experiences and the methods that we have used in our roles.

The past two years have been a whirlwind journey for us. Data is a fast-moving and an evolving environment and we get the sense that the pace of change is getting faster every month, perhaps every week. Ideas, approaches, opportunities are emerging in quick succession, there are lots of organisations in the market to recruit a CDO; relevant conferences, webinars, round tables and dinners abound. Suppliers and consultancies in the data space are pressing to demonstrate and pitch their skill and wares. The pace is both hectic and amazing. Data was an exciting place to be in 2017 and it is even more exciting in 2020!

Acknowledgements

We have met many inspiring people and we would like to thank them all. There are far too many to name every single one; but we would like to thank everyone who has taken to the stage or podium, everyone who has given up their time to participate in round tables and discussions, quite simply to our fellow data professionals who have stepped forward to share their wisdom, skill and experience – perhaps most of all to share their passion for data. We, and we are sure the whole data community, has learned so much from you. We would also like to thank the conference and event organisers, and the suppliers, who have brought the data community together on so many occasions.

After we made the decision to write this book back in November 2016, we started to write short articles about the role of the CDO and published them weekly. The purpose of this was to test our ideas in the community of our peers and to gauge if there was any demand for the book. We would like to thank everyone who read the articles and commented on them. We were overwhelmed by your support and engagement, and you spurred us on to transform the short articles into this book. We felt compelled to update the book for you because so much has changed in the world of data in three years and it seemed only fitting to reflect that thinking in a new edition for you.

We do need to pick out a few people and organisations that have helped us shape our thinking around this book, have supported its production and those that have contributed small or large pieces. First we would like to thank all our colleagues and friends who have provided quotes or snippets; we have tried to attribute each one. If we have missed anyone we apologise unreservedly and mistakes are ours alone. More specifically we would like to thank the following for their contributions.

Adrian Wyman for his absolutely fantastic cartoons which introduce each chapter: we think they bring them to life for you.

Hilary McLellan for your support and thinking around authenticity, emotional intelligence and the impact that has on the CDO.

Emma Corbett who is generous with her ideas, critical thinking and unwavering support.

Alex Young who has continued to work with me (Peter) over the past few years and has always been constructive and honest in his criticism and challenge and has always kept me true and helped to bring the ideas alive with his tireless work.

Aidan Carruthers for all the diagrams.

The team at CILIP and Facet Publishing for their hard work and continuing support.

From Peter:

Personally I would like to thank my colleagues at The Pensions Regulator, Southern Water and now Legal & General who have allowed and encouraged me to go on this journey. I must also thank Jenny Heller for her constant support for my obsession with data and the huge amount of travel and long hours over the past three years. For her enthusiasm, wonderfully creative ideas and good sense that have helped with this and many other projects.

From Caroline:

As ever the thoughts and ideas for our writing come from a hive mind, we are so grateful to everyone who shares their stories, experiences and effort with us. I really hope you all recognise what a source of inspiration and support you all are. I'm blessed with an awesome family who are all slightly mad and incredibly supportive – I really could not do what I do without you!

The night Peter and I stood on that stage at Big Data London and launched the first edition of this book to the world was one of the most bitter-sweet days I can possibly imagine. Writing has always been a passion of mine so to tell everyone that it was published and ready to be dissected was thrilling and nerve-wracking and excitingly out of my comfort zone so I was sky high. At the same time my mum was incredibly ill and while she had desperately wanted to be there, found the journey simply impossible. Instead, to make her part of the day, my sisters travelled over 300 miles to be there and facetimed the whole presentation to her and Dad curled up together in bed at home. She was my inspiration, an all-round awesome human being and the originator of 'Put your big girl knickers on and carry on!' So thanks Mum for just being incredible.

About the authors

Caroline Carruthers

Caroline is a data expert and co-founder of data consultancy firm Carruthers and Jackson. She was one of the first women to take on the role of Chief Data Officer in the UK public sector for Network Rail. Caroline has authored several best-selling books on the role of data in organisations and now consults with public, private and charity sector organisations on how to get the most out of their data. In 2020 Caroline was named 'Entrepreneur of the Year' at the *Computing* Rising Star Awards.

Peter Jackson

Peter is co-founder of Carruthers and Jackson and Director, Group Data Sciences at Legal & General. Previously he was Chief Data Officer at Southern Water and prior to that, Head of Data at The Pensions Regulator (TPR), which regulates the pensions and automatic enrolment in the UK. Before joining TPR, Peter spent 17 years providing data strategy consultancy across the not-for-profit sector, financial services and FMCG, working with large multinational organisations and blue chip brands. Peter is a specialist in data strategy, data technologies, master data management strategies, data governance frameworks, GDPR and data science strategies. Peter is the co-author of *The Chief Data Officer's Playbook* (2017) and *Data-Driven Business Transformation* (2019). He is an international speaker on data, innovation and business transformation.

Glossary of technical terms

Analytics The discovery, communication and interpretation of meaningful patterns in data.

Assurance Activities to measure confidence in a given process, framework or data set.

Audit An exercise to determine compliance against governance documents and policies.

Big Data Data sets that are so large and complex that traditional software can't deal with them efficiently. It has 'big' characteristics of three of the five 'V's of data: volume, variety and velocity (the other two being veracity and value).

C-Suite A member of the leadership team. Traditionally the titles of these roles start with 'Chief', such as Chief Data Officer.

Compliance Adherence to requirements such as regulatory, governance or other requirements.

Conceptual data model Hides the internal details of physical storage and targets entities, data type, relationships and constraints and is closely linked to business processes. The highest, the least detailed and the least granular element of the hierarchy of data models: physical/logical/conceptual. See also Logical data model and Physical data model.

CxO (Chief x Officer) is a short-hand way of collectively describing the C-level of an organisation, whose jobs typically start with Chief or have Director in the title such as Chief Finance Officer or Chief Executive Officer.

Dashboarding Making sense of your information by utilising a dashboard so you can visualise key information.

Data Data is a fact and a base component. Data on its own doesn't give you very much, as it is a fact without context; it is a raw material which needs to be processed in order to be useful. 42 is a piece of data but without knowing the context you can't do anything with it.

Data architecture One of the four enterprise architectures: a discipline focused on the models and policies that describe how data is structured, looked after and used.

Data cleansing The process of detecting and correcting corrupt or inaccurate records.

Data dictionary A catalogue and definition of all data elements.

Data governance The processes and framework which ensure that important data assets are managed appropriately.

Data lake A single source or store of all the data within an organisation, often held as unstructured data.

Data lineage Describes where the data comes from, what happens to it and where it moves over time, often mapped between systems, applications or data stores.

Data maturity Where your organisation is in terms of its data usage and where it could be.

Data migration The process of transferring data between storage types or systems.

Data warehouse A central repository of integrated data from disparate sources.

Digital The electronic technology that generates and processes data.

Enterprise architecture Made up of four architectures: application, business, data and system. It is a practice for analysing, designing, planning and implementing enterprise-wide changes.

FCDO First-generation Chief Data Officer – see Chapter 12.

GDPR The General Data Protection Regulations.

Information is derived from data; it is data which has been manipulated into something useful.

Information architecture A discipline focused on the design and organisation of information.

Logical data model Schema of a particular problem domain or business process expressed independently of a particular database storage system but in terms of structures such as relational tables and columns, object classes or XML tags. Part of the hierarchy of data models physical/logical/conceptual. See also Physical data model and Conceptual data model.

Master data A single source of common data used across multiple processes.

Master data management Curating and managing the master data to ensure its quality.

Metadata Data that provides information about other data, such as how long it is valid for and where, when and how it was created.

Physical data model This shows all table structures, including column name, column data type, column constraints, primary key, foreign key and relationships between tables. The lowest, the most detailed and the most granular element of the hierarchy of data models physical/logical/conceptual. See also Logical data model and Conceptual data model.

Proof of Concepts (PoC) A pilot project which demonstrates if something is feasible.

SaaS (Software as a Service) Where software is used on a licenced basis and hosted externally by a third party.

SCDO A second-generation Chief Data Officer – see Chapter 12.

Silo Where a department or group do not share information.

Stakeholder Someone (or a group) who is affected by a project or event in an organisation.

TCDO A third-generation Chief Data Officer – see Chapter 12.

Technical design authority (TDA) provides technical assurance across all projects.

1
The accidental entrepreneur

You know those dreams you have when you are a kid, before you realise that the moon isn't made of cheese and there is only so much your dad and superglue can fix? Well, for me one of those dreams was to be an author. Putting words down on paper has always felt more like a joy than a job (until you get to the editing process and please don't get me started on that). I have to be honest and say that *The Chief Data Officer's Playbook* isn't the kind of book that young me envisaged writing. However, the night we had our book launch was literally one of the proudest moments of my working life.

It all started at a data conference - where else? When Peter and I were talking at a conference about writing a book together I assumed that the suggestion would be one of those great ideas that fade in the light of the real world. Only this one didn't, it became a persistent thought that would lead me and Peter down a path neither one of us would foresee. That book became *The Chief Data Officer's Playbook*, which was our summation of all the things a CDO needed to know, and it resonated with so many of our colleagues and future data leaders that we were humbled by the response to it. We realised that we had missed something. It was great that the first book was a data book for data leaders, but what about the other leaders? Hence we wrote our second book, *Data Driven Business Transformation*, to help spread the message. Then the world shifted so fast in the data space we felt compelled to update *The Chief Data Officer's Playbook* (the book you have in your hands, in case you were wondering) to make sure that it stayed relevant to the world around us.

Somewhere along the line we were asked for advice from people and companies that we really wanted to help, but with us both in full-time employment it was literally impossible to help everyone and still do a decent job for the people who were paying us, so we knew something had to change. Peter and I have an awfully wonderful habit of feeding ideas off each other and jumping into deep water, and so the idea of 'Carruthers & Jackson' as a company was born. (Actually, the idea of a company was born, the name came about because I won the coin toss!)

It's been around two years since I left the safety of full-time employment in order to run our business, while Peter works full time as an awesome data leader (but don't tell him I said that, as his head is big enough already), but it wasn't until I did an interview about a year in and was asked what it felt like to be an entrepreneur that it struck me that I was one. That hadn't formed my thinking at all; I had been so focused on what I needed to do (anyone who knows me can tell you I can be a little driven when I get focused on something), indeed on what I felt compelled to do, that I hadn't realised I had jumped off a massive cliff - I'd just been too busy swimming.

My head was so full of the possibilities of what we could be that I didn't stop to focus but effectively set up three companies (because why wouldn't you?!): a data consultancy so we could help the organisations who were asking for our help, delivering practically on the advice we give in our books to help transform businesses of all kinds; a data conference called 'Datatalks', which is focused on the positive future that data can bring and inspiring leaders to help create it; as well as the education wing to spread data literacy at all levels.

Now it is only right and proper to stop for a moment to explain that no one starts a business on their own. As well as having Peter with me, I have had a literal army of support around me and could not have done it without them. My family should go without saying, but I am going to say it anyway: they have been fabulous. Emma Corbett was the first hire I made and she has been a blessing, a brilliant sounding board who is happy to tell me when she thinks I'm talking nonsense (which is hardly ever ...) and a pillar of strength when needed. Jez and Matt from Eden Smith were there for me from the start, setting up the consultancy, and have been on an awesome journey with me already! These are just some of the awesome characters who have made a massive difference to the success of Carruthers & Jackson.

The following are some of my highlights, of which there have been many:

- Receiving some documents to review from one of the first organisations we went in to help. When we first started we worked with them on their data journey and created a data strategy and roadmap for them. We have continued to do a few days' coaching each month to keep them on track. I looked at the documents and compared them to what I had first read a year ago and couldn't wipe the smile off my face. The comparison was like night and day, to see how far they had come on their data maturity journey. I did and still do feel like a very proud parent.
- Being at a conference where I heard my own voice (that is an interesting one, trust me) and turned around to see my face on a giant screen behind me. I'm so pleased that there was no one there to take my picture; I think I would have looked like the typical rabbit-in-the-headlights pose! I had just finished developing a set of data literacy courses with QA Consulting, ranging from an online basic course through to helping executives understand the value of data and what they can do with it, and I hadn't even see the completed outputs. QA had loved the videos I had done as part of the basic data literacy course so much that they were using snippets from them to showcase their courses, hence why I was looking at a huge screen with my face on it talking to the crowd.

- Standing on stage at my own conference where, over the years we have discussed everything from data and Neanderthals, through Edison torturing animals to make a point about AC electricity, to the importance of small data. We have had the audience in tears and a standing ovation (yes, at a data conference).
- Working with public and private sector organisations in four continents (I'll leave you to figure out which ones I haven't taken Carruthers & Jackson to yet). We have worked with organisations of 100 people and multinational corporates, and it is all the people who come to us as recommendations from people we have already worked with that makes me so proud.
- Meeting the graduates from the Chief Data Officer Summer School. Summer School is a free course we run once a year (over the summer, in case the clue in the title isn't clear) and is our way of spreading knowledge and helping to connect current and future data leaders so they can learn not only from us but from each other. I literally get goosebumps every time someone introduces themselves and tells me they are one of our graduates. Seeing the graduates move into data leader roles again makes me the proudest work parent that ever lived. I do put blood, sweat and passion into what I do, and to see it working with people growing into or enhancing themselves as data leaders makes it all worth it.
- Delivering a lecture with Peter on the Orient Express after spending a few days in Venice – I had to pinch myself to believe I was actually doing that one. In fact, we gave a presentation on the Orient Express as it travelled under the Alps. Peter stood there still like he was standing on a rock and I was slightly less steady on my feet (I'm clumsy at the best of times) and at one point he had to grab hold of my arm to stop me falling onto the piano.
- Getting bitten by a lion (it was a lion cub, well 10 months old, but don't let that ruin the story. It sounds better when I say I was bitten by a lion). While I was in Johannesburg to speak at a conference with Peter we went to a wildlife park. The day was literally amazing, with one of the most beautiful backdrops in nature I have ever witnessed and beautiful, incredible creatures roaming in their natural habitat. Who knew being a data cheerleader would take me there?!

Lows – I'm a glass nearly full kind of person, so I don't really dwell on the not so good stuff, but I do like to learn from it.

There have been times when I literally felt I was too busy to breathe, and that isn't good for anyone. It's so true that no matter how much you do in a start-up there is always more to do. I have had to learn to prioritise – and quickly – when what I really wanted to do was everything. I'm the type of personality that thrives on having lots to do and loves change; when I get like that, then something has to give. I have learned to prioritise and share the workload a bit.

You need to understand that there is a big difference between what people say and what will actually happen. They aren't being disingenuous in most cases, rather, thinking out loud. So you have to make sure that you have a clear understanding and signed commitments before carrying out work or thinking you have a handle on what is really going to happen.

It's a sad fact that big companies are terrible at paying on time. For them it's no big deal, but for a smaller company it can be a very big deal, and at one point early on it was a very, very big deal to me personally. Thankfully, it all came good in the end and this lack of speed in paying up has been factored into my thinking. I still don't like it, but I can work with it.

So, how does working with multiple clients differ from being an internal data leader?

People really do listen more to external consultants. Yes, I know it is annoying when you have been saying something for what feels like forever and you can never seem to get that traction – and then a consultant swans in and utters the same words and people act like it's a revelation. I have credibility from the books and speaking on the radio, but I love working with the internal teams, who normally deserve more credit than they get on a day-to-day basis. I get it, I really do. I also talk to my clients about it, the team that I am working with, as they normally have some brilliant ideas and some things they know will make a difference, so we can work together to blend all the messages together to get them what they really need. A lot of what I do focuses on transparency, and it's important to be transparent yourself, to be honest about this sort of thing happening and to use it to your advantage. Working together as a matrix team combines expertise about your organisation and a much wider perspective to help you see things that sometimes you can be too close to.

The other side of this is that sometimes things can seem like an overwhelming problem and it's easier to put the rock back in place than to try to fix what is underneath. One of the things we have focused on is helping to deliver real, tangible, pragmatic value, and - while this is an old cliché, it's still extremely relevant - helping people to eat the elephant one bite at a time. The real trick, however, is not the first bite, but knowing where to start, and that's why it's worth working from a perspective that has had to start a lot of different elephants. I never make the mistake of just assuming I have all the answers; that would just be plain hubris. It's important to get to know the organisations and the people, but I have a bigger 'bag of tricks' to dip into, since I have started (and completed) a large number of data transformations.

Acting as a challenging friend means that I can tell you things that maybe you don't find terribly comfortable about your organisation. My job isn't on the line (yes, the consulting wing of the business makes our money, but one of our guiding principles is about 'doing the right thing' even if that means walking away, telling you that someone else can do a piece of the job better, or basically just telling you how it is because you need to hear the bad as well as the good). That means that I get to tell the uncomfortable truth sometimes - not to be harsh, but to hold the mirror up and help you understand where you are, so that you can change for the better.

Conversely, I find that organisations do tend to be very negative about themselves. Sometimes when we first run workshops it can feel like a therapy session; we have to remind you to think about the good as well as the bits you want to change. We haven't worked anywhere yet where there wasn't at least a flame of something positive just waiting to be fanned. It can just be hard to see that when you are living in it, and that's a part of what I get to do that I really love - finding the hidden data cheerleaders and giving them a voice.

I get to work with some phenomenal people, teams and organisations. For someone like me who loves to solve problems, being able to get involved and help, I don't think there is a better role out there. While it's great to be considered an expert, you can never know every single thing and I absorb knowledge constantly. I learn from every question I am asked and from each nuance to every problem we tackle. It helps to make me better, which in turn helps you. I can draw from a wealth of broad sector and industry experience to help you get to where you need to be, faster, and that is just exciting to me.

So, back to being an accidental entrepreneur. I wouldn't change it for the world. I am so pleased that I didn't realise what I was doing and think about all the things that could have gone wrong, otherwise I might not have jumped. I can't wait to see what comes next: hopefully, many more organisations to help with improving their data maturity and data strategy; making sustainable change achievable; many more summer school graduates; and, most importantly, many more data cheerleaders.

If you'd indulge me I'd also like to offer some advice to anyone who would like to follow on a similar path. As the title of this chapter implies, I didn't have a career plan that meant I wanted to be an entrepreneur, and I still have conversations with my son about not knowing what I want to be when I grow up; so if you are one of those people who have a plan laid out and you know what you want, then I salute you. I find that awe inspiring and something that I could simply not do.

What has driven me is the desire to solve problems; and to solve different problems I have always needed to know more, to have more pieces of different jigsaws to blend together into different solution pictures.

Some people would describe the desire to constantly strive to know more as being that of a lifelong learner, but I'm not a fan of that phrase. 'Learning' makes you think of cold classrooms, being forced to read textbooks and write on chalkboards (for those of a certain age!). But that's not what that thirst for knowledge feels like. When I seek out new information, I feel like I'm exploring. I read, listen, watch. Then I try, inevitably fail, and learn from my mistakes. The most important lesson I ever learned was to explore knowledge with anyone who is generous enough to share it with me.

The rather eclectic mix of books on my bedside table reflects the best piece of advice I could give to anyone: let your curiosity lead! Early on in my career, I tried to fit in and learn how people did things by simply following their lead and their orthodoxies. But then I found that the most effective way to really progress and perfect your skills is to understand things at your own pace and let a thirst for knowledge lead your development.

Career development shouldn't be linear. How can you know what you're good at if you don't try new things? On my bookshelf I've got books on psychology and food, business practice and fiction. Just because you've found something you're good at, it doesn't mean you should forego all of your other interests. You shouldn't allow yourself to settle for something. Rather, you should always be looking to expand your knowledge and branch out into new areas. This will help your career to progress, but it will also help you progress as a well-rounded person.

So, my advice to anyone is, don't limit yourself. Never be afraid to wander a different path or let your curiosity lead you somewhere unexpected. Knowledge is knowledge, and even if it's not obviously useful today, it could be a game changer further down the line.

2
A reflection on the first 300 days

As we talk about the first 100 and 300 days and I have completed this cycle a few times now, I thought sharing what I have learnt during the more recent iterations would be useful. A while ago I found that the LinkedIn algorithm had been sending out notices to my friends and colleagues informing them that I was celebrating my first anniversary at Southern Water. First, thank you to everyone who sent me best wishes on this event; and second, it was a celebration. I thoroughly enjoyed my first year at Southern Water, a fascinating and exciting place to work, which is going through many positive changes. For me as Southern Water's first CDO it was a challenging year, full of opportunity and learning.

It was a busy year. It now seems odd to reflect that halfway through the year the first edition of *The Chief Data Officer's Playbook* was published and I am now writing a chapter in the second edition. Several of the chapters in the first edition were pertinent to my first year at Southern Water:

Chapter 3 The first 100 days
Chapter 4 Delivering a data strategy in the cauldron of BAU
Chapter 5 Avoiding the hype cycle
Chapter 8 Building the Chief Data Officer team

One of the key things a new CDO should do at the end of the first 100 days, before they embark on the next 300 days, is to reflect. So here goes.

My first reflection is that things (change/transformation, call it what you will) take time. By that I mean some things do have their own natural pace, whether that is procurement, technical delivery or perhaps most significantly cultural change. The cultural change is most important, because this is the thing that builds the data vision/data strategy. The story of the vision has to be repeated throughout the business and that takes time – there is the natural rhythm of booking meetings, getting into people's calendars, management meetings, leadership meetings, board meetings ... and then the story has to be understood and adopted ... and then repeated over and over again. It takes time to understand how a business works as an organisation, and also to understand what a business does. I was not from the water sector, or from utilities, so I had a lot to learn, and learn quickly. So, my first learning is that however fast and hard you might want to deliver the data strategy and start to deliver business value it will take time. So, be ready to be frustrated. The lesson from this is to relax ... a little ... at the same time as maintaining the energy and drive, if that is possible.

The second reflection concerns the hype cycle. In this chapter we speak about the importance of maintaining the pace and adding business value to avoid the 'trough of disillusionment' that can kick into the business after the honeymoon period is over. This is very true. But I have discovered a new dimension to this. It is important to manage the hype cycle within your own data team. I joined Southern Water and described the vision of the new data future to the data team, but it is important to maintain their enthusiasm and buy-in (because success will depend on them) while you get into the nitty-gritty of growing and developing capability. Your own team must not become the ones who are disillusioned because you aren't delivering the great new data future fast enough. They might not understand or have visibility of the struggles with budget, procurement, human resources (HR), governance process, etc., etc., or all the multiple distractions that mean there aren't enough hours in the day.

My third reflection is the importance of having a great team. I was very lucky at Southern Water with the skill, experience and ability of the people who have joined the data team. I was also lucky to have recruited a first-class leadership team. The power of good hires is not to be underestimated. People drive change and solve problems.

Finally, my fourth reflection is the importance of creating the data vision and building this into a narrative that can be delivered up and down and across the business. The other thing that I have learned is not only the importance of creating this narrative but the vital importance of communicating out to the business the progress towards the vision. I firmly believe that this can't be overdone. In many ways all of my reflections are interrelated, which is no surprise.

So, what did we achieve in that first year? There were three main threads to the data strategy, which aligns with the narrative in the book, and we managed to start delivering a data strategy while in the cauldron of business-as-usual (BAU).

The first thread was the data team transformation. The transformation objective was to consolidate and centralise our data and reporting functions to be more efficient and effective and break down the data and reporting silos across the business. The seven key deliverables were:

1   a common source of 'mastered' and governed data
2   common standards of reporting and techniques
3   a centre of excellence and support to the business
4   a centre for data science and advanced analytics
5   alignment of the data strategy with the information technology (IT) strategy
6   provision of quality and assured data for our regulators
7   GDPR (General Data Protection Regulation) compliance.

This required a significant shift of people and activity from across the business into the data team and a significant change in the ways of working.

The second thread was an immediate data strategy (IDS) to address the burning platforms and hot issues and to add immediate business value. In this first year the new data team on-boarded new data technology and started to roll out new browser-based dashboards, removing the dependency on spreadsheets for reporting; improved data management, quality and assurance; started some data science projects; provided data analytics to deliver cost savings and business efficiencies; and has provided data support to an Ops Excellence Programme, PR19 (the water sector Price Review 2019 submitted to OFWAT) and Target 100 (a consumer water consumption target). This was a sizeable delivery, bearing in mind that it didn't get underway until five months in (I was listening, thinking and building the team and the strategy for the first five months). These deliveries have been achieved while the data team was maintaining BAU activities. The wheels had to stay on the bus, the marathon runner had to keep running.

The third thread was to develop a target data strategy (TDS), which continued to evolve alongside the IDS over the next two years as we approached the start of AMP7 (Asset Management Plan 7) in 2020. The TDS was a platform for transformation, innovation and collaboration which the data team began with The DataWell, a cross-sector initiative to share data and create open data sets working across the water industry in the UK.

Looking back at the end of the first year, the data team at Southern Water achieved a huge amount. This was only possible because the new team had a positive approach and took on the challenges, was well led by the managers and leaders in the team and received full executive sponsorship, which was fundamental.

So, at the end of another two years in the role as a CDO, what are my reflections and observations now, mid-2020?

First, I think that data has risen up the agenda even further. I think that there is a growing realisation that organisations will fall into one of three buckets during the course of the fourth industrial revolution. There will be the leaders, the followers and those that go into decline. Once an organisation sets its sights on being a leader, or at least securing its place as a close follower, then the data awareness trigger is pulled and the hunt starts for a CDO. So, on reflection, the conversation over the past three years has not quietened down; in fact, it has become hotter and more informed. I think it is also interesting that the conversations about data are now broadening out beyond the 'data' community; data is a conversation and subject that is being picked up at other chief officer conferences and in vertical-specific conferences and debates. The conversation is now wider than just between data leaders; it is extending to our colleagues in the C-Suite. More people are talking about data, and in a more informed way.

It is interesting writing this chapter during the COVID-19 lockdown. The terrible pandemic has made everyone more aware of the importance of data, the importance of collecting data, of collecting the right data at the right time and of the many different ways that the same data can be used to tell different stories, depending upon the agenda. Even before the current pandemic, events involving Cambridge Analytica, Facebook, social engineering, data breaches have pushed data up everyone's agenda. So, I think data has risen up the agenda for most organisations and will continue to do so for the foreseeable future.

Second, as an active CDO with skin in the game I have a number of further observations:

1   The importance of communications comes home to me again and again. To deliver a successful data strategy and a growth in data maturity there has to be a massive shift in the organisation's data culture, data literacy has to improve, and a key part of this has to be communications. This has come home to me time and again over the past two years. Don't be afraid to recount the success stories of other organisations, perhaps even to invite them in to talk about DataOps and data technology or data governance. It can make it seem more real. After all, you may well be talking about things that are quite alien to your organisation.

2   Over the past two years the importance of data governance has come high on my agenda. I would caveat that with 'appropriate' data governance. I would not wish to boil the ocean, but I would go after the critical data elements (CDEs), get these under governance and the rest will follow. This will also bring the rest of the organisation along on the journey, because getting the CDEs under control will help everyone.

3   We have talked about data strategies needing to be flexible and organic, in fact it was Leslie Titcombe, the then CEO of The Pensions Regulator (TPR), who told me that the TPR data strategy

needed to be flexible to cope with the changing regulatory environment. I am even more convinced of this, especially in large organisations where one data strategy will not fit all parts of the business. So, the macro-data strategy should focus on establishing the core data principles and best practice to be followed across the organisation and fit these into a data vision for the whole organisation that can then be interpreted in detail in the separate parts of the business but is aligned to the core principles of the strategy.

4   I have also learned to seek out the good. The initial data landscape isn't always a landscape of bad and negativity. There will be pockets, or large areas, of good data practice and activity. Embrace these, celebrate them and shape your data strategy around them, or at least 'grandfather' them into your visions. This will provide you with a massive head start. Also seek out those parts of the organisation that are ready and willing to innovate and try new things. The appetite and ability to do this will vary enormously across a large organisation.

5   You will need to find a way to remain a visionary and evangelist at the same time as getting close to the weeds. Stakeholders will expect you to provide the strategic view, map out a plan for the future, but they will also expect execution. You will need to become a 'talker' and a 'doer'. I think the danger is to become too 'consultative'. You have to remember that you have got skin in the game and you, yes you, need to make this change.

6   Over the past two years we have witnessed the rise and rise of DataOps, hopefully because we wrote about it at some length in our *Data Driven Business Transformation* in 2019. I am now even more convinced that DataOps is the way forward and delivers significant results at pace. Changing an organisation to incorporate this into their operating model is a challenge; people won't understand what you are talking about; you will need to recruit or up-skill and it creates a whole new, much-needed discipline in the business.

Creating a full capability DataOps team will deliver more to business, more quickly, than a team of data scientists. Of course data scientists are an essential part of the full capability DataOps team.

7   Partially linked to the point above about DataOps is the need to get the right data technology on board as quickly as possible if it isn't already within the organisation. There are some bits of kit that you just need, and that will enable new ways of working. Often, having the right technology will make your budget go further.

8   Access to data is imperative. Without this, the value-creation side of the role is all but impossible. I heard a presentation by a fellow CDO who was recounting a story of his experience; he asked his IT colleagues for access to the data so that he could meet the demands upon him for advanced analytics, a simple conversation:

'Can I have access to the data, so that I can do my job?'
'Yes, of course! Which bits do you want and we'll get them ready for you.'
'Uh? No I want access to all the data, and all the time.'

This is something that organisations need to get with very quickly. It will constrain any chance they have of becoming data driven or data enabled if the data is locked away. Surely access to the data is a fundamental business need?

9   My final two observations/reflections relate to the people element of the transformation process. Remind yourself to take the pulse of those near to you, or, rather, ask them to check your pulse. Your direct reports should be a good sounding board and advice for you. They will see and hear things going on that you aren't aware of. Listen to them. Don't get so busy that you don't have time for them. Your peers will probably give you good insight: is your message landing, do THEY understand what you are talking about and can they see your vision? And, finally, listen for the signals coming from your boss or senior stakeholders, don't be 'so right' or 'so adamant' that you can't hear them.

10 Resilience. Again, I know we have discussed this before, but you have to be ready for two steps forward, one step back. Most importantly, you have to be ready for being blindsided; you think you have landed a message and have moved on, only for a couple of weeks later someone to ask the question again or make a decision that clearly demonstrates that the message didn't land. That is the time for resilience. Also, be ready for those occasions

when your brilliant ideas are discounted and dismissed, only for them to be represented by someone else later as their ideas, and now the ideas are embraced as just what is needed. That is the time for resilience and realising that the good of the organisation is more important than you and that the adoption of good ideas, regardless of who lands them, is the most important thing. It takes a while for people to 'get' data.

11 The final thing that I have learned in this past year, which all of my colleagues have learned as well, is to be ready to adapt at pace to the unexpected. COVID-19 has tested many businesses, and I am sure that it will have tested many data strategies.

3
Why does any organisation need a Chief Data Officer?

Introduction

This chapter is aimed at all parts of our audience: the CDO, the data community, C-Suite colleagues, business owners and recruiters. So the 'you' in this chapter is everyone. We put forward some scenarios that many of you will recognise and some symptoms to look for. Not all CDOs will be successful, so we try to get to the bottom of why some will fail and, linked to this, how to measure the success of a CDO. Perhaps most importantly, once an organisation has realised that it needs a CDO and has recruited, how do you get the best out of the CDO? We believe that this chapter is ever more relevant now in 2020. The case for the CDO is now emphatic, and an increasing number of organisations have appointed a CDO over the past three years; but even where this has happened the question still gets asked 'do we need a CDO?' Understanding who is asking this question and why is now very important. Even though more CDOs are being appointed there are some organisations which are still to get there. Why is this and what will be the consequences?

Why organisations need a CDO

So why does any organisation need a CDO? If a CDO is hired at the right level, it will be a big investment and they aren't going to just come on their own; they will bring a team of some sort, even sourced from positions within the organisation, they will cause disruption and potentially add cost, and the company got along just fine without one before. Right? Some of the core capabilities required in a CDO team are not present in many organisations. This is especially true of the senior roles, such as head of DataOps, head of data governance, chief data architect. Many of the other functions and more hands-on roles may well be filled in the team by the redeployment of existing data-literate people or up-skilling existing staff. A CDO who is tasked to leverage insight and value from the data will also wish to recruit data scientists.

Did the organisation get along just fine before the CDO? Well of course they did or they wouldn't be in business. However, in the data revolution, the fourth industrial revolution, businesses will fall into one of three types. The leaders, who will embrace data and set themselves up for success; the followers, who will be late adopters of data strategies, and the laggers, who will not make the data move – and we have all seen examples of what happens to that category. We are in that phase when most organisations are at the tipping point of making the decision. They have or will appoint a CDO and set them up for success; or they won't, and the future won't be bright for them. For strong businesses that decide that they don't need a CDO, that they are just fine and have managed without one, it may take a while for the consequences of that decision to materialise. Do any of the following scenarios happen in your organisation?

- After completing a long and complex project you complete a lessons learned exercise, exposing the pain of mistakes that have cost you time and effort in order to ensure you never repeat those mistakes again. You even try to remember the parts you did well in order to look at how you can improve, and you diligently write it all up into a lessons learned report and file it in the best place you can think of. A year or less down the line you are involved with another project similar to the last and find the exact same mistakes that you wrote down in black and white, only the organisation (the business) never read your lessons learned report because they couldn't find it. The lesson was never 'learned', only filed. This is the best-case scenario – perhaps there never was a lessons learned exercise.

- You end up sorting out the data issues at the end of a project because data cleansing and data migration were only an afterthought and spreadsheets were used instead of proper ETL (extraction, transformation and load) tools, etc. This 'after-project' cleansing of data can suck up huge resources and time and have commercial impacts.

- You have the world's most intricate spreadsheet, it is truly a thing of wonder with thousands of lines in it, and if you put your new data in very specific places then you very nearly get what you want out of it. It's not quite right, but close enough, and with a little bit of manual manipulation you have what you need. You can't change the spreadsheet to do what you actually need, as you don't understand it. The lovely gentleman who created it left a long time ago and writing the documentation to explain the spreadsheet was not part of his job. Or the spreadsheet started to fall over and stop working as more and more data was entered, or the version of MS Excel is no longer supported, etc., and everyone has begun using their own spreadsheet with no version control.

- Your lovely financial system allows you to search on different criteria because it has flexibility built in and you wanted it to be easy to use, but when you have a query about an employee's expenses you discover you are getting widely different results depending on which analyst integrates the system. The eureka moment comes when you realise that the employee is actually known by their middle name but is filed on the system by their first name, so while 'Frank Smith' has never claimed any expenses 'Henry Frank Smith' is not quite following company policy!

- You need a new shiny IT system. You have decided that it's worth the investment to be able to share your data and information in a more collaborative fashion but you are keen that you don't lose the really good data that is in the legacy systems; you can't find any of it but you are sure that is just because the system is old and creaking, so by putting the data into a new system it will all be better. The sales team explains what the total cost of ownership is and you are good to go until that very sensible person in your IT department explains how much it will cost to move all of your data from the old system into the new one, and it amounts to more than your nice new IT package is going to cost to implement and run.
- Or you want to replace applications in your IT stack but you've got no idea of the data lineage between applications or the upstream or downstream data impact of replacing a single application.
- Data is stuck in silos within business units or departments across the organisation and there is no way to effectively share data.
- Your CEO wants to run a data-driven organisation, getting better engagement with customers, reducing customer churn by understanding and predicting their needs better, or increasing business efficiency, or perhaps he just wants a better corporate dashboard to help with decision making.
- Perhaps your data analysts or teams preparing reports are spending most of their time sorting out data issues rather than analysing or reporting.

If any of this sounds familiar, then you are not alone. This is happening across all large, complex organisations which have not placed enough emphasis on the management of their data and information.

We now have access to more data than ever before. The estimate of how much data we held across the world in 2018 was around 4.4 zettabytes (to put this into context, in 2009 the entire world wide web was about half a zettabyte in size). According to the IDC in 2025 this will have grown to 175 zettabytes (if you had to store that amount of data on DVDs there would be enough of them to circle the world 222 times) so data is continuing to grow at an accelerating rate. We have all become hoarders when it comes to facts and figures. If you could represent organisations as a TV show, most companies would be that programme that shows people who need help because they have filled their houses so full that they can't live there comfortably any more: 'SoS Data Hoarder'.

We have convinced ourselves that because it doesn't cost us much to keep it, why not keep it all – just in case? You never know when it might come in useful. The sheer volume of what we have has convinced us that it has no value. Only having so much of it means that not only can we not see the wood for the trees, we don't value the wood any more. Our data has become meaningless at a time when we could do more with it than ever before.

The drive for cloud, for Big Data in the cloud, is now being questioned. Is it cheaper, is it better? Cloud-first strategies aren't necessarily the brainchild or hobby horse of the CDO. Often they are proposed for financial reasons (seldom for security reasons, which is both odd and disappointing). A cloud-first strategy does not de facto deliver the aims of the CDO. Often cloud leads to data hoarding: 'let's stick everything into the cloud', 'let's get Big Data and we can face the future'. It can actually undermine the aims of the CDO: hoarding isn't good, there can be a lack of data governance and access to the data may not be any easier than before, when it was in legacy systems. What the CDO wants is governed data that the business can access quickly and can understand and trust. Too often, cloud-first delivers the opposite. Does this sound familiar?

We live in a value-conscious world, there is not a company around that does not have some limit on finances and resources, and we continue with the same mistakes. If we have limited resources, why are we wasting them collecting data that has no value for us other than the boasting rights of how many petabytes our company stores? If we keep blindly collecting data and expect different outcomes, then we are insane.

If you continue the wood analogy, we have literally lost our path. We have lost the focus on why we are collecting data; it has become an exercise in its own right rather than a means to an end. We have fallen into the trap of saying 'we need it' rather than asking *why* we need it. What are we hoping to get from it, and what benefits can we derive from it? What are we going to get from it, and why do it in the first place? The question has become more than 'Why do we need it?' We also need to ask 'Why are we migrating it? Why are we copying it?'

This can be further illustrated by the concept of the information value chain: how does the information you use link into the value chain of the organisation? What end result are you expecting, and what do you need in order to get there? This isn't just about using the five whys; don't stop at five, start asking questions and don't stop. The focus has to be on delivery and benefit. If you are collecting or storing data and the data doesn't deliver benefit, stop doing it. Keep your limited resources focused on doing what gives you benefits. The CDO gives this clarity and direction to your attention. Also focus on collecting smaller data sets really well, on governing them and maintaining their quality and standard, rather than on thinking more is better. Quality is better than quantity. Accessible quality is better than quantity.

Data governance

Have you heard about big data and do you love the idea of getting all that wonderful insight that will turn you into the next internet or digital sensation? We have all heard stories about the amazing benefits companies can derive from jumping onto the latest data bandwagon. Big data features in TV shows as the scientific way of using a crystal ball to predict the future, and if the media tells us it's true, it must be true. Many organisations are still searching for the 'digital nirvana'; they want to shift their interactions with their customers and clients into a digital or self-service space. This has many drivers: they believe it is what the customer wants and expects; they see it as a route to reducing the costs of service, or a way to reducing errors and speeding up service by straight-through processing; or the COVID-19 pandemic may have demonstrated that it is needed and will make them more resilient.

Does a data lake sound like a compelling way to fix all of your company's problems? You've been sold on understanding what the future will bring just by understanding your past – it can't be that much effort, as you already have all the data, it's simply a case of using it. You can't trust the data you already have, but if you put it in a shiny new system or platform, then all will be well, a technological miracle will happen and the data will be cleaned by magic, never to wander off target again.

It isn't enough to go halfway on this journey, either. Moving from an instinct-based decision-making method across your organisation to using your data to back-up your instincts isn't going to yield the types of step forward that you will be expecting from the introduction of the CDO and his or her helpers.

You might need a data lake, you might need to get the beneficial insights that big data can give you, and you could use your family silver (data) to create a wonderful transformation, but, as the saying goes, 'garbage in, garbage out'. It is important to know where and when to use new tools and techniques, otherwise you will potentially disrupt your organisation without reaping any benefit from the action. Again, this is the guidance your CDO will provide for you. They will accelerate you through one part of your data and digital transformation, and slow you down when that is the right thing to do.

All of this is before you stop and look at the small mistakes that are happening on a daily basis across your company that, when added up, are costing the company time and money that you don't want to waste. So many business processes are made inefficient by 'data friction'. To give you a simple example: someone in your sales department enters the wrong company name in the billing name field on the customer relationship management (CRM) system such as ACME Ltd rather than ACME (UK) Ltd, an invoice is raised on 90-day payment terms for the wrong company and you don't find out until day 89. So, because the sales team made a tiny error it has cost the company 90 days' cash flow. This simple example demonstrates how your reputation can be damaged because you staked your reputation on flawed data that you were convinced was right.

To avoid such flaws, you definitely need governed data. A small governed data puddle will be far more use to you than a large, contaminated data swamp. The problem with the contamination is that while you know there are small pockets of data that you can't trust, you don't know which bits you can trust, therefore you don't trust any of it. So, you are making decisions based on poor information, you are taking too long to make decisions because you know you can't trust your data, you are wasting money replicating a process to check the results, or you are stagnant. With governed data, at least you know what parts you can trust, you know that you don't have to replicate anything, you know the accuracy rating of what you are reviewing and can take that into account when you make a decision. Data friction is reduced.

If there is no single, big, easy reason to convince you to hire your first CDO, there are a million small ones that are happening every day in your company – those are the real reasons why you should hire a CDO.

The value of a CDO

The chief data officer is the voice of data within a company and represents data as a strategic business asset. Company data is very valuable. In fact, one could argue that there is a very real exchange rate between data and profits, whether you use data intelligently to increase efficiency, increase sales or create new business opportunities entirely. Deeper insight into customer relations, decisions, the market and so on is of tremendous value. To empower IDG Sweden by giving us that insight in an actionable manner – through technology, workflow, visibility and compliance – is my ultimate goal.

(Henric Jogin, IDG Sweden)

The CDO gives cross-organisation vision and strategy for data for the first time, and if this all sounds like a culture change then you are right. We know that in some areas 'culture change' can be considered dirty words, but anything that gets an organisation thinking differently is a culture change. One person will not be able to deliver the change needed to get the best from your data; a team of people, whether small or large, will feel like they are climbing Mount Everest as they try to get every single person in your company understanding why your data is important and treating it accordingly. Only when the company works together with the CDO and their team do you have a task that is starting to look a lot easier.

Why do CDOs fail?

If it is such a good idea to get a CDO into your organisation, why is Gartner (a leading research and advisory company) predicting that 50% of CDOs will fail, and how do you stop that happening in your company? Investing in a new role can be risky, so knowing why CDOs typically fail and avoiding those mistakes can only be a good thing. There are myriad reasons why people fail in roles, but trying not to fall into one of these traps can set up your CDO to succeed.

- **Absolution.** Hiring a CDO doesn't absolve the rest of the company from looking after the data; it doesn't suddenly become the CDO's problem so that you don't need to worry about it. The CDO is your focus point, not the person suddenly accountable for all data across your company. The organisation will need data owners and data stewards from the business.
- **Culture change.** The CDO is a disruptive role and not everyone or every company adapts to change well. In order to adapt to the new way of working which the CDO will bring, numerous functions across the business will need to change. Obviously this will need to be managed carefully, with forethought and understanding, but change has to be expected. If you don't want to change, don't hire a CDO.
- **Company culture.** If you have a culture where no mistake is tolerated, then, again, don't hire a CDO. The role starts off creating your solid data platform but bleeds into innovation, and that's where the saying 'If you aren't making mistakes you aren't trying hard enough' comes in. Innovation involves making mistakes. A CDO will drive innovation, so if your organisation has a culture that does not tolerate mistakes, then a CDO may not be for you. Many organisations do not fully understand the risks that they face caused by data and 'old' ways of managing and processing data; data needs to be understood from a risk point of view.
- **Expectations** from the role. We talk about the hype cycle later (Chapter 7), but it is worth a mention here. Expectations vary widely with the CDO role and we are slowly coming to an understanding of what we can expect from our new, shiny hire, but don't expect world peace solved in the first week followed by eradicating cancer in the second. You know what you get with a Chief Financial Officer or Chief Information Officer, but don't assume that every problem you have can be put into a bucket and handed over to the CDO – a little bit of realism will go a long way. It is important that organisations truly understand the scale of the challenge.
- **Level of the role.** Just giving someone a chief-level title but putting them ten levels down in the organisation doesn't work. This role drives an enterprise-level change across your business. As well as their having the necessary leadership abilities you need

to put them in a position where they have decision-making authority and can get across the business.

- **Restrictions**. As well as considering the level at which you place the CDO in your company, what restrictions you place on them need to be carefully negotiated before they come on board. If you only want to get to a governed data state but that's all, and that's what works for your company – great. Tell your CDO before you hire them, because they may be coming in to really drive an enterprise data strategy in the truest sense and not be terribly happy with doing what they will see as only half a job. There's also the catch-22 element to this process: if you know you need a CDO, how did you get into that position? Do you already have a data strategy in place, such that there are limits on the investment, resources, priorities, etc. that you will give your CDO, meaning the job is less transformative and hence less appealing for a pioneer, or are you so flexible that you will bring in a CDO without knowing what they are going to do? This is almost a chicken-and-egg scenario: do you need a CDO to tell you that you need a CDO and all that brings with it? Rather than get too philosophical, this ultimately comes down to flexibility; having a starting point is great, but you may have to expect it to flex.
- **Experience**. As with any role, there is a certain level of experience you should expect from your new CDO. However, in the current climate this is poorly defined and there couldn't be a bigger pool of experience vying for this role. We would recommend that you seek some help to make sure your job description is practical and reflective of what your business needs and your expectations, to make sure you get the right candidate who works for you.
- **Is your IT king** and averse to being challenged? Or does your company have a relationship with an existing outsourced supplier which is locked rigid? Or are you swamped by legacy technology which is all out of support? If so, you need tactical solutions which might detract from your future strategy.
- **Budget**. Finally this may seem like an obvious call out, but over the past two years evidence has shown that some organisations, even though they have brought a CDO on board, haven't invested enough in the function. Many organisations are faced with many years of under-investment in their data, there is no data

governance and a lack of data skills within the organisation. To move the dial on this requires investment.

When you have your lovely new CDO, what do you do with them?

Before you hire your nice, new data cheerleader for the organisation there are a few questions your company needs to ask itself.

1   What do you want them to achieve? (Hopefully this book can give you a few hints and tips on that score, and if not this one, then perhaps our book *Data Driven Business Transformation*.)
2   Where are you going to put them?
3   How high up in the organisation do you place them?
4   Are you going to invest in data?

You need to have an idea about the answer to question 1 before you decide the answer to any of the other three questions. Your answers to these three questions will have a big impact on the scope and reach of your CDO. The best CDO on the planet will not be able to elicit a transformational change if they are stuck in the technology basement of your company where they are lucky to see the daylight of your front-line business.

> . . . an eye opener for all organisations who seek to 'invent' posts for outcomes they can't yet conceive. For me it's about using the data to tell a story (whatever your exploitation outputs might be). And I might need to tell the same story twice (or a thousand times), but I want the story to reliably contain all the fundamental elements that make it believable. A CDO develops an organisation's data story; the rest will become the organisation's history.
>
> (Johanna Hutchinson, Head of Data, The Pensions Regulator)

One of the main things to address is the confusion caused by the similarity between the Chief Information Officer (CIO) and CDO titles. While there are obvious synergies between data and information (you literally cannot have information without data), there is not currently the same clarity between the roles. A natural mistake in companies has been to place the CDO under the CIO because data and information are believed to be the same thing (more on that later). The CIO title grew from the need to lead information technology, and possibly we dropped the wrong word from 'information technology' in order to create a three-letter acronym. So, basically, we are stuck with imperfect titles which don't quite reflect the purpose of the two roles. It's also entirely possible that you can have a CIO who covers both roles, the Chief Technology Officer (CTO) and CDO, and really is your CIO; however, in large, complex organisations, looking after the IT is normally a big enough job in its own right. Lots of CIOs are welcoming the help they get from a CDO. An intelligent supplier (CIO) works better with an intelligent customer (CDO). It is very important to fully understand and define these roles for your organisation.

The other problem that we face with the management of data and information is that the 'business' tends to believe it is not their problem; it is the role of the CIO and their department to take care of all of that for them. By separating the two functions and aligning the CDO with the business you embed the idea that the data is the business's problem, and therefore everyone's responsibility.

Initially, the placement of the CDO within an organisation depended a great deal on internal politics. While this is something that happens with every new role it isn't a sustainable model going forward. People naturally move around companies and you don't want to reorganise or face the pain of losing valuable corporate knowledge when personalities don't get along. It is important to know where and why to place your CDO within the organisation.

There is no hard-and-fast definition of exactly where the role should be placed, as it is dependent on the type of company you are part of and the primary role of the organisation. The one very clear rule when placing your CDO role is that it must be in a business function which allows the CDO to work across the whole company. Data doesn't understand boundaries; data flows and permeates through every crevice in your business, you can't limit it to a silo and you don't want to limit your CDO if you want to get the best value from them. You also don't want them to sit in a silo, in case the other silos decide that the only way to be equal is to create their own CDO with another name just to keep things interesting.

The level of the CDO role also depends on the type of organisation you are and what you want to be. Worth considering here is that where you place the CDO role in your organisation demonstrates the value you place on data within your company. As this discussion has shown, thinking about where you put the CDO role in your organisation needs careful consideration; there are pros and cons to wherever you put it. Broadly, you would put your CDO role into one of three places. Reporting directly to the Chief Executive does send a powerful message about how important your data is to your company and does ensure the independence of the CDO, giving them freedom to work across the business – but what will this do to the others around the top table? Reporting straight to the CIO has also been popular but is becoming less so; it does make the data management and architecture align beautifully with your IT structure and can help to leverage your data as an organisational enabler, but by putting the role within an IT function you are stuck with the age-old view that 'IT takes care of that for us', whereas looking after data is everyone's problem and responsibility. The natural place to put the role is in a cross-functional area of the business; putting it in any siloed part of the business will severely limit any ability to do the role justice. In a cross-functional position you retain the data independence and keep the cross-functional aspect of the role intact, and, as long as the relationship with IT is strong, then you can keep the alignment across the enterprise architecture. It's important that the CDO sits close to the business in an area that gives them autonomy. A lovely description of the place for the CDO is when you talk about 'IT and Operations'. The CDO looks after the 'and', forming the bridge which links it all together.

What do you measure them against?

There are roughly eight categories that current CDOs are measured on:

- data management
- data maturity of the organisation
- organisational efficiency
- business outcomes
- regulatory outcomes
- organisational agility
- profitability
- revenues.

Focusing on the first part of this list (data management and data maturity) is where your CDO gets your basics right, putting in place good data management and governance to create the solid foundation to move forward through your data journey, creating the infrastructure that you need so as to be able to proceed with innovation and agility. If you focus on the middle part (operational efficiency as well as business and regulatory outcomes), you already know that you have the basics covered and you want to exploit your data and really use it as an asset, making your business as efficient and as effective as possible while at the same time expanding the art of the possible. When you focus on the end of this list (organisational agility, profitability and revenues) you are really moving into the disruptor space, you are monetising data through new products and services and really pushing boundaries.

It is a bit too simplistic to say your focus should start at the top of the list and slowly work its way down. What about if you are a not-for-profit organisation: are you ever going to focus on revenues? You might focus on value for money as a possible measure, but it has to be right for your organisation. Some organisations try to include all of these measures in some shape or form; however, like most targets, there has to be a focus; you simply can't deliver everything at once, and in some cases the data maturity level within the organisation will dictate where your focus on this list lies. Wherever you focus, you must tie it in to your business strategy.

Celebrate your successes when you can: if you are solving real business problems, mitigating risk and adding value to an organisation, then take a little time to congratulate yourself, as you are probably succeeding. It is really important to acknowledge your successes, as you should also be implementing an enterprise-wide transformation, and these tend not to happen overnight. So, anything that you can do to break it down into bite-size chunks will make it easier to demonstrate your progress.

Chief Data Evangelist or Chief Data Enforcer? Either way the need for 'better data' (however you interpret that) is universal now and therefore so is the need to convince everyone of the importance of the governance and engineering roles . . . even when all they want is a quick data science 'hit'.

(Charlie Boundy, Head of Data Science,
UK Department for Work & Pensions)

4
The secret ingredients of a Chief Data Officer

Introduction

This chapter is mostly aimed at the CDO, to help you understand and appreciate the skills and characteristics that are required to be a CDO. However, it is also a useful chapter for organisations thinking about recruiting a CDO – what sort of skills should they be looking for? To that extent, this chapter is also useful for recruiters when trying to assess potential candidates. The chapter emphasises the necessity for the CDO to have 'narrative powers' and lists the seven secret ingredients of the CDO. It introduces for the first time in the book the concept of 'first-generation CDO' and 'second-generation CDO'. The first-generation CDOs are those taking up roles in organisations which haven't previously had a senior function responsible for data and a data strategy, whereas the second-generation CDO builds upon the firm foundation created by the first-generation CDO and generates more value for the organisation. In this second edition we also introduce the concept of the 'first-generation CDO – replayed'.

The CDO's role

> The role of the CDO is evolving fast. In one type of organisation compliance and regulation may lie behind the creation of the role, whereas in another the CDO is there as a response to business model disruption and the need to drive innovation.
>
> (Emanuela Aureli, Spencer Stuart)

Compared to most of the C-Suite colleagues, the CDO is faced with a set of unique problems. There are some similarities: the CDO is a subject specialist, and in that respect is similar to the Chief Finance Officer, Chief Investment Officer or Chief Risk Officer. The CDO also operates across the organisation and so has similarities with the Chief Operating Officer or Chief Accounting Officer. However, the CDO does have a unique set of challenges: primarily, the role is still being defined and, in the absence of certainty, there is an assumption that the role will solve all the problems the organisation is facing. The CDO in many organisations is a new role (the number of people in CDO roles doubled between 2013 to 2014, and probably doubled again in 2015 – Karl Greenberg, MediaPost 2015), while the other C-Suite executives have roles and responsibilities which the organisation recognises and understands.

The CDO is bringing a new dimension and focus to the organisation: 'data'. All organisations will have used and depended on data for a long time, but the arrival of the CDO will be the signal that the business intends to be data enabled, that data will have a new importance in the business and that it will be pivotal to the future of the business. It's great if an organisation wants to be more data driven and we will talk about motivations later. Understanding which motivations are the driving force will help you when you find yourself setting up.

> [T]he CDO role is one that is 'new', there is no blueprint and there are many differing views on what the role of the CDO actually is, hence the many challenges faced, and the ingredients needed to be successful. In my role of business development I have met with many CDOs, some of whom

demonstrate all of the attributes you have mentioned, but what never fails to amaze me is that so many of these C-Suite individuals do not hold their own purse strings and have to beg, borrow and steal budget. Surely a key ingredient to the successful CDO is complete control over their own budget?

(Roger Tomlinson, Business Development –
Data Solutions for the banking and financial services market)

Most organisations will be demonstrating poor practices and bad habits in their collection, use, storage and command of data. So the CDO will be bringing a new culture and regime. Instilling such change brings with it a level of fear.

To achieve this difficult task of changing culture across an organisation, and changing the way individuals and the business use and view their data, the CDO needs some unique qualities. The qualities of a first-generation CDO are similar to the qualities of a second-generation CDO, although with a subtly different focus. The different types of CDO will be discussed separately in a later chapter.

The importance of communicating

Communication is such a key skill that it has to be mentioned first. The ability to translate quite complex 'data' concepts and technology into the appropriate language for every level of the business, and the ability to use communication to win hearts and minds, is vitally important. The ability to 'pitch' at the right level is a critical component in the communications skill set. The CDO has to be able to communicate with the existing IT community within the organisation, to be able to communicate on a technical level, using the correct language and terms, and to understand the jargon and specialist terms coming back the other way. They will also need to be able to communicate in 'business speak' and be credible in putting together and communicating the business benefits, organisational benefits and implications and pains of the inevitable transformation that will accompany the new data world. The CDO will also need to be able to communicate with the subject experts within the business. All of which can make you feel a bit like a translator. It is much harder to make a difficult subject easy to understand than it is to make a simple one sound complex!

An important part of what a CDO brings is the ability to tell an engaging story and paint a picture with words. Articulate what the data utopia looks like that the organisation is heading towards, so that everyone can become interested in data. We know that this may be hard to believe, but some people consider data a four-letter word, they think it's dull and boring (we know, we think that's weird too). Translating things through telling stories engages people who ordinarily don't read books about data and information. Stories are like music, they paint powerful images that can bring people on a journey with you.

Whatever business you join, you can't assume that you understand it straightaway. Even if you are coming from the same industry, the business itself will be different, and you have to be able to understand the business in order to talk sensibly and coherently with people who are experts in their fields. As a CDO, your unique selling point isn't that you understand pensions or the railway better than anyone else, it's that you understand how to help an organisation get the best from its data and information. It is the same as pulling any matrix team together: the strength in the team doesn't come from everyone being the same, it comes from different expertise coming together for a common goal.

Over the past four years we have experienced this personally, joining organisations in sectors which are new to us. Rapidly, you need to be able to communicate with the subject experts in the business so as to understand their 'data needs' and their 'data pains'. This requires being able to communicate with the business about the business. Perhaps this level of flexibility in communication reflects the ability of the first-generation CDO to be a quick learner, the need to have excellent business analyst skills and, most importantly, the ability to listen and ask the right questions.

This ability to communicate is nuanced, as seen above, and there is another angle which we have experienced: moving between the private, public and regulated sectors. This must be true to an extent for anyone moving between organisations and sectors, but a CDO may be more exposed to this variety because, as a group, CDOs seem to be more mobile across sectors because of the demand for their specialist skills.

On reflection since the first edition, we believe that the ability to communicate is even more important, both projecting and listening, the ability to create messages (yes, messages) that resonate and can be understood across the organisation, up and down the organisation and outwards to partners and suppliers. It is also the ability to find the right communication channels; these may be the intranet (though the intranet may be a great place to hide news); they may be webinars, podcasts, town halls, the town halls of other functions, conferences or perhaps the use of external communications to deliver an internal message.

Think about creating a communications strategy for data and your vision. This should follow the principles of any good communications strategy, but it is important to have one. Once things get busy it is easy to forget to communicate. The strategy should not only include setting out the vision of the future; it should clearly identify the next steps and set expectations, but it should also celebrate the things which have already been achieved (and the people who delivered those achievements).

The other ingredients

The CDO needs to be a master at relationship building; they will need the support of the others in the C-Suite, and beyond, to deliver the data strategy vision. The CDO will rely on other parts of the business to deliver much of the data strategy and to deliver the message: IT to deliver the technology, Customer Support to deliver improved data entry, etc. At times the CDO will need to go toe-to-toe with colleagues, but the most effective results will be achieved through good relationships.

> There is no division where you can't add value by using data.
>
> (Davide Cervellin, Head of EU Analytics, eBay)

It is fairly inevitable that a first-generation CDO will be a catalyst for change. All successful change is built upon excellent communication and relationship building. The CDO will spend much of their time in the business building these relationships. Huge amounts of time, especially in the early days, will be spent in meetings, at boards and working groups, chatting to colleagues at all levels to build good working relationships. These relationships need to be genuine, and time spent building them is a wise investment. At all levels people in the organisation will need to respect you, listen to you, have time for you and, most of all, trust you. They must have faith in your judgement call. A crucial element of the relationship building is showing the respect to your colleagues that they deserve, and being empathetic to their situation and challenges. The business was running before the 'new' CDO arrived, people were doing their jobs and it wasn't all bad. And the new CDO will have a huge amount to learn and information to gather from these people. Essentially, the new CDO must make their colleagues feel 'supported' through the relationships. Certainly, in our experience, building the relationships has paid off in huge value: more junior colleagues feel able to share their ideas and observations with you, and senior colleagues can share their worries and concerns. This can be done only through mutual trust.

At a conference once, we were told that we were famous for our coffee and cake. We can both attest that it isn't because we bake them but, rather, because when we talked about relationship building we talked about the power of coffee and cake. The idea is that we need to put people at ease when we talk to them, for instance by finding environments that are more informal to make people feel relaxed, so that you don't depress them when you talk to them about what problems they are facing and what keeps them awake at night!

A word of warning: it will not be all plain sailing. The CDO, like all people, has to be aware of those bad relationships which aren't working and are sour. These need to be managed and resolved. Just remember that you don't need to be everyone's best friend. As the saying goes, you can please all of the people some of the time and you can please some of the people all of the time, but you cannot please all of the people all of the time. Or you can do the right thing for the organisation, knowing that sometimes you will have winners and losers but by building relationships based on respect you can still have good working relationships. You don't have to like someone and they don't have to like you, but you do need to have a good, solid working relationship; and since you're the one who needs the relationship to work, you're the one who has to work on it. Just don't be needy.

> From a data scientist's eye view looking up, a key thing for me is that the CDO sets the tone of the organisation by fostering a learning culture, and making space for innovation. I frequently see data scientists who are so focused on the pressures of business as usual, that they have no capacity to bring to bear the considerable benefits that data science can offer.
>
> (Matthew Upson, Data Scientist, UK Government Digital Service)

Apart from trust, these good relationships will be built on credibility. The new CDO must be credible to the board, colleagues and the business.

The business must trust and have confidence in the new CDO. The CDO will be leading and introducing big, new ideas, and therefore must be credible.

Much of the credibility will be founded on specialist data knowledge. The new CDO must know 'data' and have a thorough understanding of data governance, data management, data quality, data science, advanced analytics, data strategy and data technology; you must care and be passionate about these areas. Perhaps you will not need to know the detail that the data team will bring, but enough to develop the data strategy and create the bridge between the specialists and the board, the specialists and the business. In lots of cases you will be the translator, so it's not just about understanding data, the business has to feel represented too. You aren't on anyone's 'side', rather, you are on the side of the data - and it doesn't flourish in silos.

> The line that struck me was the one about a CDO must 'know data'. Evangelising about the possibilities is key to winning over the board (your point about being a good communicator), but having the bloody-minded persistence to turn a tanker across so many parts of the enterprise of which you have little or no control is hard.
>
> (Charlie Boundy, Head of Data Science,
> UK Department for Work & Pensions)

The CDO's track record from previous positions isn't enough, the credibility will have to live and breathe within the new role. You will be challenged, and this will come from many places. Colleagues in the senior management team may be sceptical about the direction of travel, or about the seemingly independent decisions that are being made; the people who are doing their jobs based on the time-honoured tradition of 'always doing it like that' will not like that you are asking them to modify what they do or how they do it - and humans are ridiculously inventive when finding ways to get back to their comfort zone. The challenge may come from quite junior individuals in the business who are fearful of the changes that they see coming and may feel threatened in their own credibility, position or job. All of these fears are real and need to be addressed.

We think that credibility is better than authority, and that authority should be delivered through credibility. In an ideal world the CDO will demonstrate great credibility, with the authority required for change being projected from above through the acknowledged support of the senior sponsors in the business. Be consistent and stay on target – the credibility will come.

> The CDO needs to be technically aware to avoid relying on others to understand the architecture that is being delivered to support your requirement. This understanding helps the CDO have more strategic conversations.
>
> (Hany Choueiri, Chief Data Officer, Bank of England)

The CDO must be the cheerleader for data and have a driving passion that convinces other people of the value of data and a good data strategy. Like all cheerleaders, the CDO must maintain a constant smile, good humour and have boundless energy. To put this in business terms, the CDO must constantly be on message. We've stopped counting the number of times we have explained master data management, either in simple terms or complex terms, because we were doing it so often. The CDO will need to explain, rationalise and deliver the message over and over again, with the same patience and with the same passion.

> Storytelling and passion are the must-have abilities for CDO.
> (George Chiu, Big Data and industry consultant in telecommunications,
> retailing and banking)

The required credibility and passion for data aligns with the need for the CDO to be resilient, to have the ability to stay on message, to stay focused, to keep the strategy in sight and to realise that losing a battle is not necessarily losing the war. In fact, changing the data culture of an organisation is a campaign and there will be many ups and downs during the course of the campaign. The CDO must not become discouraged by apparent setbacks. It is amazing how many times a message lands or an idea is finally adopted after what seems like an eternity since you first suggested it. Perhaps other things actually were a higher priority at the moment when you first suggested it, or perhaps others were shouting louder, or perhaps your message just wasn't right, or being delivered right, or being understood.

The new CDO must be able to shift gear between tactical delivery and strategic planning, for two reasons: first, because it is important that the CDO delivers incremental value to the business so as to avoid the 'hype cycle' (more of that in Chapter 7); and second, because they will need to identify the quick wins and easy fixes in the current data environment so as to stabilise and rationalise the current data environment while the data strategy is being rolled out. You will be developing the company's strategy and really getting involved in the big-picture thinking, so conveying concepts is a really big part of the role. However, if you do only this, then you are missing out. You also need to handle the highly detailed conversations about why particular metadata is important – it ties in with the credibility and the relationship building we were talking about; and you will be talking to people about the specific part of the subject that they need to talk about, demonstrating the agility you are going to be relying on heavily in this role.

Finally, the CDO will need a sprinkling of luck. They will be faced with unexpected situations, difficult people, organisational resistance, institutional muscle memory; their luck will depend on the proportions of these that they face. We have seen incredibly capable people struggle in roles because they were hit by events that we would classify as one-in-a-hundred-year events, and they were hit by three of them in a nine-month period. No one can flourish when all they are doing is fire-fighting against events that they couldn't predict in a hundred years. Let's hope that doesn't happen to you, but pack your four-leaf clover just in case you need some help from Lady Luck!

Figure 4.1 summarises the skill ingredients of a CDO and, apart from luck, their equal importance.

Skill ingredient	%
Communications	16.5
Relationship building	16.5
Specialist	16.5
Strategist / tactician	16.5
Credibility	16.5
Passion for data	16.5
Luck	1

Figure 4.1 *Skill ingredients of a Chief Data Officer*

And, before we move on, don't forget the resilience!

The note of caution in all of this is that it's the intangible that trips people up. So, spending some time developing self-knowledge, i.e. emotional awareness, behavioural awareness and non-verbal communications, is time well spent. These, when brought together, will culminate in a greater awareness of how you can maximise your impact on others and how best to adapt to different audiences while maintaining calm, clear and straightforward communication.

Finally, and this probably falls across all of the above qualities, is the ability to recruit good people. More on that in Chapter 10.

The subtle difference in the second-generation CDO is that they will need all of these ingredients and more, perhaps. The second-generation CDO will not be the new kid on the block, so they will need to have the ability to pick up where their successor finished off, and also have the ability to keep the ship and crew calm, and not fearful of yet more change. Their special skill will be the ability to add value and keep the momentum alive and the innovation flowing. It isn't as simple as 'job done, just carry on'.

I suspect that one of the pitfalls to avoid is the scenario where the organisation feels they've 'outsourced' their data challenges by assigning ownership to someone with a fancy title – they can't fire and forget everything to do with data! I would agree that the ability to have and communicate an inspiring vision is key: many of our clients aspire to be 'data driven' but don't really know what that means for them. Explaining how their operating model and roles will differ is important for clarifying both the benefits and the effort needed to realise them. Beyond that, I'm sure we've all experienced the fact (also evidenced by the earlier comments) that everyone in an organisation has their own priority: data science, data quality, data governance, upgrading archaic databases, experimenting with new tools and techniques . . . which is exactly why stakeholder management is vital. All of those are important but it's unlikely they'll all be invested in at once. So the CDO must have a keen awareness of the business strategy, and the lineage from their own road map components to the way they support business outcomes. An example from several organisations I've worked with over the year: management of customer data. Great idea, but we bumble on without really making an effort so why bother now? (Let's set aside GDPR [General

Data Protection Regulation] for a second.) Well if the business strategy says we want to be the top organisation for customer service, and calling our customers five times a day because we hold duplicate copies of them with no real management of their preferences is stopping us achieving that, then customer data management has a business case. It's why whenever I'm asked to consult on a data strategy I always ask early on: 'what is the business strategy?'

(Christopher Blood, Data Strategist, BAE Systems Applied Intelligence)

The first-generation replayed CDO is perhaps being born out of the observation from Gartner that some CDOs will fail. We have already discussed in the previous chapter why some CDOs may fail, but in those organisations where that has occurred they may decide to recruit another CDO (or data leader) because they still perceive the importance of data and their original drivers for recruiting a CDO still exist. In these circumstances we will be getting the 'first-generation replayed CDO'. They will face 'we tried this and it didn't work' again and again, so they will need to fight even harder to make change happen. What qualities are required here? Well, all of the above, but almost at a heightened level. This replayed version of the first-generation CDO will need to communicate even more, and perhaps be even better at it. Inevitably they will face the challenge of 'why will it be different this time?' They will need to be a master strategist and, of course, will need to be very credible if they are not to be written off before they start. A tough ask. But the organisation may have got its recruitment right the second time around, and they may set up the 'first generation replayed CDO' for success, so all may not be lost.

It is certainly very important to understand if you are a second-generation CDO or are, in fact, a first-generation CDO replayed.

5
The first 100 days

Introduction

This chapter looks at the importance of listening and asking questions during the first 100 days, but also filtering what you hear. The chapter explores some of the critical tasks of the first 100 days: making the 'case for change', assessing the level of data maturity, defining the destination and the scope and establishing the data basics. It is aimed at the CDO, so the 'you' in this chapter is the CDO.

There is little scarier when you are starting a new role than having a blank piece of paper in front of you. The chapter aims to help you over that hurdle. It covers what you need to focus on when you start your nice, new CDO role, how you understand where you are starting from and where you want to get to, as well as the steps to get you there. What makes a good case for change, and why is 'coffee and cake' so important? What do you need to do about your 'information basics' of governance, architecture and engagement, and what are the tangible examples of how to communicate your visions to people? Why are quick wins so important? All of these questions are covered in the first 100 days.

Starting out in your new role

> [H]aving evangelists to drive engagement with the wider organisation is key – without passionate advocates for the power (and importance) of data to the organisation, you run the risk of governance activities being 'red tape'. If staff do not implicitly understand why data is important, you will forever be trying to herd 'data cats'!
>
> (Julian Schwarzenbach, Director, Data and Process Advantage)

How do you climb Mount Everest? One step at a time. It can seem like a completely overwhelming task at times, but just by focusing on the next step you can look back at the end of your first 100 days and see how much you have achieved.

When you take on this role expect to spend a lot of money on coffee, cakes and biscuits! Such a large part of being a CDO is based on relationship building, so get ready to spend a lot of time meeting people – hence the coffee and cake budget!

Gartner predicted that by 2019, 90% of large organisations would have hired a CDO – but only 50% of these would be a success, and this seems to be what really happened. Much of what determines your success or failure going forward will take place in the first 100 days. Essentially, it is about getting the basics right now and building firm foundations for the future.

What do you expect when you start? The first 100 days are important to set the expectations for the CDO you are going to be. Now, from one (two) CDO(s) to another, expect a real rollercoaster of a ride: there will be amazing highs followed by moments where you sit with your head in your hands, wondering what on earth you have done. Basically, a microcosm of the rest of your role as a CDO has just been crammed into a shorter time period. It is important during this time not to get dragged into the weeds and set about fixing small problems, of which there will be many. Give yourself the time and space to see the big picture, to understand the scope of the task and how the business runs. We don't mean you should totally ignore the small problems – you have to demonstrate the value you can bring to the organisation, so picking some of them to solve, even putting in place a process to prioritise them, might be a win. Just don't let yourself be so overwhelmed by them that they become your focus rather than solving the big problem that stops or inhibits them from happening in the first place.

It is also important during the first 100 days to understand just what sort of CDO the organisation wants. Does this line up against what you were told during the recruitment process?

Pre-work

There's a bit of what we would call prep work that you need to do before you really get stuck in. It's almost your pre-basics, and you can't skimp on the time you put in to this. You need to understand the business. Now we know that almost goes without saying but we're a bit pedantic, so we're going to talk about it anyway. There are only two ways into the role, from inside the company or from outside. Obviously, if you are from inside the company you will have a bit of an advantage here, but don't fall back on your laurels; make sure you still do your homework on the organisation, as you might be surprised by what you can find out. If you come from inside the company you more than likely came from a siloed part of the business (based on the fact that the majority of any business is siloed!), which means you will have preconceptions about the other areas. Let's not start the role by assuming anything.

If you come from outside, you should have a level of data awareness, otherwise why would they have offered you the role? So you should know that understanding what you are getting yourself into is pretty fundamental. The focus has to be on understanding not only what the business does but how it does it, how it is currently treating its data, and the current level of understanding about what value it has. This can start to give you some insights into what is going wrong with the data and where you can start to add value.

So, start by listening, listening and listening; and when you think you are done with that, listen some more. Don't ask questions about the data – to be honest, as we have said before, data is a bit of a four-letter word for most people in the business. We may care about the difference between data and information, or the value in well-placed metadata, but that's probably not how the rest of the business sees the world.

Ask your peers, and anyone else you can, to find the time to share a coffee with you, and ask them what problems they are facing, what keeps them awake at night and what they are really proud of. In other words, use language they would use and ask them lots of nice, open questions that let them talk to you about their priorities. People naturally gravitate towards the data and information problems they are having because they are aware of what your title is, but you can find some real gems in the areas they don't even realise are data related. You will be truly amazed by how many big, company-wide problems are really data related somewhere near the root cause. Everyone in a company is busy, but directors, especially, are really busy people; however, they will happily talk to you about the shopping list of things that they need done to help them. A few prompts about business processes can often be useful: How easy is your regulatory reporting? How do you provide reports to your clients? Are your business processes documented? How easy is it to do ad hoc reporting? If you want to get a bit more into the data you can ask questions like: Can you get easy access to the data you need? How often and why do you use spreadsheets in X or Y business process? Do you manage or manipulate data in spreadsheets? And if you really want to have a data conversation perhaps ask questions about data catalogues or data dictionaries or data lineage. These sorts of questions will tell you a huge amount about the current level of data maturity in the organisation.

Two other things that you need to be aware of while you are investing your fortune in coffee and cake: first is the politics in play. Every organisation has politics in some shape or form: you might not need to take part but you definitely need to understand it; it will help you to avoid any verbal landmines and also could lead you to find some important sponsors/stakeholders out in the business who are worth focusing on. The second is the need to filter the information you are getting through the importance filter. Is something really on fire, or is it just smouldering while London is burning behind it? Is it someone's pet hate and could fixing it produce a much larger gain in credibility? How strategic is it – will it take a long time to fix or can it be a quick win? These are all things that you need to factor in to your planning.

Ah yes, we used the 'planning' word. We're not suggesting that you come up with a 1,000-line Gantt chart (but if that floats your boat, then carry on), but let's not pretend that you can complete a journey without a map of some description. Your first plan probably won't be pretty and it will change, but it will show you the next step to take when you have lost your way.

While you are meeting with all these stakeholders, find out what the heartbeat of the organisation is, what pattern there is to meetings, what crucial meetings you need to be part of and make sure you stay plugged in to. Basically, what makes the company run? Seek out the gateways that control and manage 'change' and get data involved as part of those gateways. Where are people trying to do the right thing with data, and can you help each other out?

Finally, a word of warning: in the words of Laocoon, 'Beware of Greeks bearing gifts'. You may get unexpected offers of help, or someone may suggest a quick route to the solutions. Consider these carefully. You should ask yourself, 'If it is such a good idea and so obvious, why hasn't it been tried already?' or, 'If the answers are already known, why is there such a data mess?' Be critical, quietly (remember to build those relationships). Alternatively, what looks like a nice, attractive Trojan Horse and a good place to start may be a can of worms and drag you into those weeds that you will never escape from. We apologise for the mixed metaphors but they do work together in this context.

We know this probably sounds like a great deal of pre-basics, but we are coming to the end of the list and they are all really critical! Finally, make sure you understand your procurement and finance processes. Many a slip-up in a project has happened because the right process was not followed, and finance has those checks and balances in there for a reason. So, while you might want to rail against them, you aren't going to win any friends that way and by following the process from the outset things will go a lot smoother.

The case for change

So, now that you have covered your pre-basics the very first thing you need to start doing in your new role is to understand your organisation's case for change. If it's not there, create it; if there is one and it needs help, redefine it. But whatever you do, make sure you have a clear, easy-to-describe case for change. In order to be an effective CDO you will be changing the organisation, and no change starts better than with a burning platform or an absolutely massive benefit delivered quickly. If you can't establish the case for change, then you might as well go home at this point; without it you are doomed to poor results or outright failure. An obvious case for change, and often a very good starting point is the 'R' word, Risk. Is data presenting an unacceptable risk to the business? Does the business really understand the risks presented by its data? If the 'R' word isn't going to work, and it normally does in a good many cases, look for an audit report that has looked at data. Are there outstanding audit actions? But don't make it all negative, balance this with the positive benefits that will naturally flow. It's just that starting on that side of the spectrum normally highlights some tangible outcomes that will start the ball rolling.

The case for change helps you to define the vision of what benefits you are aiming for, whether they are saving the organisation from repeating mistakes or gaining insight to derive more value. It's the compelling argument that makes people want to help create the future you are selling. It also helps you to define your scope and start to set expectations about what you will and won't be doing. People often forget about the 'not doing' part of a scope, but it is just as important as what you are doing, if not more so: without it, people can overlay their own expectations and just assume they are getting everything they've always wanted, just because they have misinterpreted what you meant. While you need to create a compelling vision, it's best to be realistic about where you can go, what it will feel like and how long it is going to take to make a difference. A key tip, as well as making the scope fit the budget: only the fortunate few have the budget to fit the scope. It is important to communicate what can and can't be done within the budget and resources, so be clear and consistent in how you talk about this. Be honest, otherwise you are setting yourself up to fail.

What makes a compelling case for change in the world of data?

First, you need to check your understanding of the problem. Is it something that just you or a small group is facing, or do you have more company-wide, systemic problems? It is very likely that if the root causes of the issues you are facing are data related, then it will be a company-wide problem, as data affects every single part of your organisation. You will see issues like not sharing data, not having one source of the data (or data that works together), no one treating the data as an asset, people repeating work because they can't find something that has already been completed . . . this list can go on and on.

Gather your advocates around: if you have checked that other parts of your organisation are facing similar problems that you can trace back to similar causes, then you should have others in your corner who understand the value of data and why things need to change. This really helps, because you will have a lot of persuading to do to win over the company to get things moving, so take any help you can get.

Articulate your case: what are the problems you are trying to solve, and what is the wonderful data utopia you are going to create? What is your big picture? Make this a nice, simple, consistent message; if you have all these advocates helping you, then you need them all to be saying the same thing. Confusion is not going to help you convince anyone that you know what you are doing. There has to be a single voice heard, no matter who is speaking. Reduce your message to the elevator pitch, come up with five or six key principles. Make it easy for people to hum along and start to make it a catchy tune.

Maturity model

It might be helpful to look at the level of data maturity of the organisation, which you can factor in to where you are going to make improvements. It can also give you a baseline to demonstrate what you have been doing and where you have made a difference. The first time you run a maturity assessment you will need to include as many stakeholders as you can, so as to get an unbiased view of as much of the organisation as possible. It will be time-intensive, as you will need to spend time helping people through the questions and to understand why they are spending their time giving you this information. As the maturity of the organisation grows, you can use this information to form part of your assurance process and benchmarking activities, as well as to tailor your approach to your work ahead. The company will not need a full assessment every year, as that is potentially too intensive for an organisation to undertake, but a few well-placed self-assessments can ensure that you stay on target.

You will need to address the following questions to your organisation when compiling your maturity model:

- **Strategy**. Mature organisations communicate the leadership's way forward with a business strategy to inform and provide the principles for detailed strategies relating to key areas of the business, of which your information strategy should be one.
- **Leadership**. Do the leadership demonstrate that they make data-driven decisions, or do they hide behind endless dashboards and reports?
- **Corporate governance**. Are the key elements of good corporate governance in place and are they well deployed? Do they operate in isolation from each other or ensure that a well-rounded approach is taken? Are relevant and tailorable assurance activities regularly undertaken and well used?
- **Framework**. Does the organisation have the right framework in place to make the rest of your pieces hang together? How do you bring policies up to date and make sure you keep them that way?
- **Policies**. Do you have the relevant policies, standards, procedures, etc., to make sure you are setting up the people within your organisation to succeed? Are your instructions clear, consistent and easy to use? Do you have a framework in place to demonstrate the interrelation between your policies?
- **Information risk**. Is information risk well defined, and at what level? Do you understand your business criticality? Are the tools in place to help manage and mitigate this appropriately? Do you really understand all the data risks – re-work, poor decision making, fraud?
- **Architecture**. Do you understand how information is used across your organisation, how it cuts across silos? Have you mapped the architectures out? Who is accountable for which bits?
- **Organisation, roles and responsibility**. Are roles clear and agreed across the organisation? Do you have a team dedicated to being the data cheerleaders for the organisation? Have roles been defined to address elements of information management and assurance within the different domains? Do you have a steering

board in place which is empowered to make data- and information-related decisions? Are training programmes in place for both your data and information professionals and the wider organisation?

- **Metrics**. Are you measuring progress and performance, and reporting benefits at a corporate level? And are you measuring the right things to drive the kinds of behaviour that you want to see in a data-valuing culture?
- **Skills**. How skilled are your teams – not just your data teams, but the rest of the organisation? Do they have the right data literacy skills to be able to take advantage of your data?
- **Behaviour**. Do you value your data and understand what it can do for you? One indication of this is how much money you have spent on it over what time period. Has it been underinvested, or has it been well invested but not succeeded, and why not?
- **Tools**. Last, but definitely not least, do the tools you have access to help you or hinder you? How many data-related systems are you currently using, and are people using them for the right thing? Do you understand the information life cycle within your organisation?

One indicator that you probably won't find in a maturity assessment, but will help to form your thinking, is to find out why the company is deciding to put a CDO in place now, if you are the first one, or what the previous incumbent has faced, if you're not.

Having some set of metrics to help you understand each level in the maturity assessment means that you can replicate this after a period of time. Then you can (hopefully) demonstrate progress and it will help you to identify the areas you need to focus on next. Typically, any kind of measure that takes you from 'totally useless' to 'totally awesome', with a few steps in between, will give you the level of detail that you need in order to demonstrate your organisation's maturity in these areas. Aim for no more than five or six levels, otherwise you will spend ages arguing about what category different parts of the business sit in, rather than solving the big problems you are trying to get them focused on.

A data maturity assessment will give you a point of departure for your data strategy. We have found that having a credible data maturity assessment in the bag that will stand up to scrutiny, that has been derived from conversations with the business, can and will be used over and again as the starting point for your data story. If you can deliver the findings and outcomes of your data maturity assessment and get those understood and accepted by senior management, the executive committee or board, so much the better, as this will then become a constant point of reference and justification. Make sure when delivering the feedback and outcomes of the data maturity assessment to include pertinent, strong and water-tight examples. Bearing in mind that you've spent 100 days talking to a lot of people, make sure that you gather and test these examples.

Don't forget to stress the urgency of the situation as well. Organisations are being pulled in so many different directions: why do they need to put their limited resources and budget into solving this problem now, when it has lasted in this state for years? Without a sense of urgency this will be dropped down the list of important things to do and probably never see the light of day. If the sense of urgency isn't going to fly, try the idea that 'fixing the data' is foundational to every other endeavour and ambition of the business, and support this with use cases and examples.

Next on the list is that you will need plenty of facts to back-up your big-picture story. Don't underestimate how much time you will need to spend with senior stakeholders in order to understand the problems they are facing, gaining tangible examples from them of where poor data management is affecting them or where great opportunities are being missed – and which are personal to them. If you can deliver a little shock value here, you can normally extrapolate some big potential savings from your knowledge of how things are in existing day-to-day activities. Don't say anything that you don't believe, but be brave and talk about the cost-saving potential. In some cases the numbers may look so big at this early stage that they are unbelievable. Remember that a lot of blood, sweat and tears will be needed to achieve the big savings, but they are possible.

Lastly, it's lots of listening, talking and listening again. You just can't beat talking to people. As the saying goes, we have two ears and one mouth and should use them accordingly. Make sure you listen, and hone your case for change until it is indisputable.

Vision and strategy

While the compelling case for change tends to focus on the downside of life (unless you are a disruptor and have a genius idea to leapfrog your business forward), the balance comes in the form of your vision and strategy. At this early stage you should be able to come up with a good strategy that is high level and visionary. There are so many different variations of a good vision, but something memorable, concise and meaningful to your business is what you should be aiming for.

There is no point in starting a journey without having an idea of your destination. You don't need a fixed point that you are trying to drag the company to; rather, have an idea in mind of where you are leading them. It's a bit like giving them a treasure map where you may not have buried the treasure yet, but you know which island you are burying it on and they will get more maps, the closer to the goal they get.

Your strategy ties in to the vision to create that utopian data future for your business; however, at this point you probably don't know enough to create a strategy in detail. Spending more time with the business, understanding what causes it pain and what will make the biggest difference to it is needed before you finalise your strategy. At this point possessing a broad understanding will be enough to get you going. The more you include other stakeholders in the work, the more likely it is that they will buy in when the work really starts. You also need your team to help you with this so that they also feel invested in it. The building blocks of your engagement journey start here.

Including items like accountabilities will definitely help you, as there is nothing more guaranteed to cause problems downstream than poor understanding of who is accountable for what. This is especially the case since this is a new role, and people will believe that you are taking something away from them. Whether this actually is the case or not, it needs to be addressed in a mature and careful fashion. Alternatively, there will be gaps where no one steps forward to be accountable; at least by raising the issue of accountability gaps and helping the business to understand why they cause a problem you can promote the right accountability debate.

Next you will need to clarify the scope of what you are covering. Data is a massive area for any organisation and if you are not careful you could find yourself trying to boil the ocean. Setting out what you are focusing on and why, as well as defining the broad scope for now and in the future, will help understanding grow as to what you are bringing to the company. Something like the POTI (Process, Organisation, Technology and Information) model is a good tool to use and covers the basic areas that you need to understand so as to make sure you have a high-level direction for what you are setting up.

Briefly, the POTI model covers the following:

- **Process.** Highlight any operational business models that will have to be changed. As you are creating a new department this is highly likely to be an area you will need to pay some attention to: what will be different, how will it interact with the rest of the organisation and how will you make changes to the existing structure in order to put the new one in place?
- **Organisation.** This area addresses the people changes again. If you are creating a new department from this exercise you will need to define it carefully. What is your aim for the new department? Are you looking to bring in all new people from outside the organisation or blend outside skills with the development of current staff, giving them the chance to enhance and grow their skill set?
- **Technology.** This gives you the tools to do your job well and is closely linked to the data flow through the company – but don't assume that you are suddenly in charge of the IT department (you aren't). Let them do their job well so that you can do your job well. Focus on the end state you are trying to get to and work with your IT department to understand how they can get you there. Provide the picture – let them put the jigsaw together in the right way.
- **Information.** Ordinarily, when you are starting out on something new and create your POTI model the area that is not completed in the same way as the others is the information area. This area is nearly impossible to define and something suitably high level and unmanageable is entered; however, you can really go to town here. Lay the foundations for your information and data strategy for the organisation.

We are going to assume that you have a team in place and that you don't have to do that in your first 100 days, knowing how long this process can take. There is a need to have people around you to help, as no one person will ever be able to change the company without a lot of support. Apart from the need for skills and experience that are varied and wide-ranging, you will also need the support when you have some of your rollercoaster lows, to help you get back on the upward track. It is worth noting that if you do inherit some sort of team you will probably want to reshape it and reskill the team. A new target operating model for data will almost certainly be a part of your data strategy. If you don't inherit a team, then during those first 100 days your mind will be working through the sort of team, its shape and skills, that you will need in order to deliver your data strategy.

So, you have a team (or are planning one), a case for change, a vision and the makings of a strategy. Now you need to look at what basics you are trying to get right, what materials are going to make up your foundation.

What are your 'data basics'?

To keep it simple we've broken these down into three main areas. There is more than one way to achieve the following basics and you need to find out what works for you, but we have included examples of ways to progress in each area.

Governance

Let's face it, you will be making changes to the organisation and you might not always get it right first time - remember the old saying, 'If you never make a mistake you aren't trying hard enough!' So, what must be in place is a way of letting people know what is expected of them, what they are really accountable for - be that policies, standards, procedures or whatever your company uses to help everyone understand their responsibilities, as well as a control mechanism for managing those policies. How do you make decisions on how the organisation needs to treat its data and information? Who is involved in this process? And, if you are smart, you will get people involved who cover large parts of your company.

The steps to this are simple, but don't underestimate how long they will take; writing a policy is easy, but getting people to sign it off can take a considerable amount of time and effort. The following will give you the set of steps needed to put together a plan for this area; how much you get done is dependent on how mature the organisation is already when it comes to governance, and the willingness and readiness of people to change.

The first thing you need to focus on is finding out what state you are currently in; gather together anything you could call a governance document. This could be anything from a standard to a 'how-to' guide; it is any existing process and whom it touches, as well as any decision-making bodies that cover governance in the data space. Have a look at what you have; the chances are that you will have overlaps, inconsistencies and gaping holes in your guidance, so it's not really a wonder that people weren't treating the data as an asset – they were probably really confused about what you wanted them to do with it. Now that you have pulled it all together, develop a map of how you are going to sort it out; figure out what you want it to cover, and perform a gap analysis in order to see how much effort you need to devote to this area.

We find it helpful to create a guidance tree diagram (see Figure 5.1), where you have the most basic instructions you want everyone to know at the very highest level and then break this down into the different sections you cover within the data domain in your organisation. Keep each level very simple, concise and easy to understand, but in a way that you can keep dropping down a level of detail until you get the amount of information that you need to do your job on the area where you need it. In this way you won't produce a vast document that will

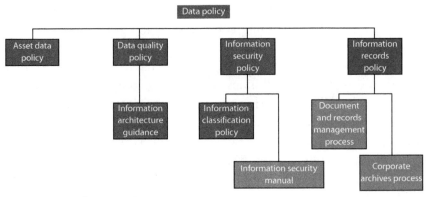

Figure 5.1 *Guidance Tree Diagram*

be the next cure for insomnia and you should make it easier for people to get to the information that is relevant to them when they need it.

At this stage we wouldn't be too worried about how it looks – that is something you can put into your longer-term plan. Right now it is more important that you have a set of guidelines that are easy to use, rather than making sure they are all on the same template.

Creating something like the guidance tree diagram is also a building block for when you start to do the education and training for the organisation, as it gives you the basics in each area and the different components you need to focus on when you are looking at how you break down your training offering for the organisation.

The next thing to worry about is how to get sign-off for all these guidance documents and how to make sure that they are all kept up to date. This will probably be two separate processes, as you are drawing together a new community, so it's highly unlikely that you already have the right meetings or stakeholder group set up to sign these off, and what you start with may not be what you need in the longer term. Be open to change with this process, especially.

At first just getting the tree diagram and the plan approved to a point where you have a clear mandate is important. This isn't about whether or not you have the right level of authority but it is an important activity that encourages early buy-in. If you are the new player on the block you will need the interaction of the existing players to help them to understand what you are doing and how it will impact other people and departments.

In your plan you also need to reflect on what your review cycle is. It will seem like you have all the time in the world to worry about updating these guidance documents; after all, you have only just created them and they have to be okay for a while. That little while will slip through your fingers quicker than you can imagine, and without a gentle reminder that you need to look at them again it will be easy to forget about them and focus on the more day-to-day concerns of the role. That is not to suggest that they will need a full rework every two years – we are aiming for a level of consistency here, so we would hope that is not the case. However, it can be surprising how little things can slip over time. What if you define a role in a governance document that doesn't really gain traction within your company and you end up morphing the responsibilities into some other roles or places? How is someone who is reading the document for the first time supposed to know that? It's just a good housekeeping principle to keep these documents up to date, and a review plan will help you do that.

Going forward, you will also need to allow for different governance streams; for instance, the people who are desperately keen on information architecture conversations may not be the people who want to look into the detail of your records management policy. Having smaller, focused groups who report to a decision-making body which has the appropriate level of authority will break down the tasks, so no one should be sitting in a meeting that bores them.

Look at what type of governance works for your company and copy the relevant parts of it (there is no point reinventing the wheel!). Just make sure that you have adequate coverage across your company. Look at areas like the highest-level information domains in your information architecture (see the next section): who is accountable for each of those domains, and might they be good representatives to have on your decision-making body? What are the different areas within your business which look at the different architecture models (your IT department, especially, will have different types of architects)? Bring them together so that any changes to the information architecture are reflected in other levels where appropriate.

Creating a 'heartbeat' of how things happen and are progressed will help your team and the organisation to find a rhythm in how they work together. All of this will help with your engagement activities.

Information architecture

Next, let's look at your information architecture – not the vast swathes of detail that sit in your data dictionary (at least not at this point), but the big headings. What are the top headings (perhaps five to ten) which describe all the information in your company and (most importantly) who is the one person who could make a decision on each one? You might also refer to this as your 'data domains'. This is not about playing the blame game; that just makes individuals hide from any kind of accountability and leads to a kind of company-wide whack-a-mole game. Remember the quote from above: 'If you aren't making mistakes . . .? Your information domain owners (or data domain owners) are accountable experts in their fields who understand specific areas of information within your business and can give firm direction and decisions in their area. Once you have the highest conceptual level agreed, then it's time to move on to the next level, adding richer detail as you go. Don't expect this to ever be complete – it will always morph, but it should be a firm foundation for better decisions about your information and the use of it. You will find that data domain owners will be more prepared to take on the role, and the challenge, if you are clear about what is expected, why they should do this, and then provide them with the correct training and tools.

Engagement

Last and definitely not least, how are you going to engage with the company? Where is your network of evangelists coming from who will sell your message? It's great that you know who can make decisions about the data and that you have clear instructions for how people should treat your company's data, but it really is pointless unless you tell them. Naturally we are talking about mass, company-wide e-mails, which of course everyone reads every detail of, inwardly digests and then miraculously and immediately changes their behaviour . . . in our dreams! This is hearts and minds time here: what is your compelling argument for change; how are you making their life better; and what is in it for them that makes it worth changing their behaviour? At the very least tell them what you expect from them. This is where your communications strategy comes into play.

Working with willing volunteers and enthusiastic amateurs will always outperform press-ganged experts any day. Try to get champions across the business who will give you good coverage and are well regarded in their own areas. When it comes to getting the message out, having people working with you and to whom other people in their department will listen can make a world of difference. However, if you do have the press-ganged variety of 'volunteers' this can also work to your advantage: while they are much harder to bring over to your side at first, when you do convert them they will be the strongest advocates you can have. It is better to mobilise many small armies than to try to raise one big army. The smaller armies dispersed across the business will spread the message more quickly and more widely.

Get all that right, and at least you will know you have covered your basics while you start your journey.

Quick wins

The next thing you have to do is to get some value from all of this quickly. One hundred days will pass by in the blink of an eye for you, but the business has invested in you and will want to see some return on their investment. Have you found any tactical quick wins you can put in place? You will need to find something that demonstrates the value you can get from your data early on. You have the vision, the people and an idea of the data architecture – put them to use to find some quick wins to show the organisation why it's worth working with you. Don't expect to deliver any of these during your first 100 days, but certainly have a few good candidates up your sleeve for the next phase, and have some idea of how you are going to deliver them.

> Being in the CxO group doesn't mean avoiding politics and other more established CxO roles may have the power to hamper your intentions. So wouldn't it work better to agree some form of plan, remit or funding before you sign on, similar to how commercial service providers work? Your points around the case for change ring very true though. I've had some great breakthrough moments where a client has asked for some specific help with a data problem and through early consultancy have been able to turn that into a clear statement of the impact of the problem on the organisation's bottom line, thereby giving both the immediate client and their own stakeholders clarity on why effort and support is needed. If you can manage to do that the case and buy-in starts building quickly. GDPR is helping too: the risk of new, massive fines is starting to build the case for solving data management problems that organisations have let slide for years. There is a counter-argument though: discovery and experimentation can often have no known business outcome at the start. It is investment which might have to be written off if the discovery is that something won't work or won't add value. That's a bolder choice for an organisation to make, but one which can be transformational.
>
> (Christopher Blood, Data Strategist, BAE Systems Applied Intelligence)

6
Delivering a data strategy in the cauldron of BAU

Introduction

This chapter begins by painting a picture of BAU (business as usual), what the 'data environment' looks like at day zero when the first CDO arrives, and understanding who is currently making the data decisions, or how and why they are being made. The chapter then puts forward the case for a dual-track approach to a data strategy – the immediate data strategy and the target data strategy – with six tips for success and the idea of fixing forward.

> We have a Chief Data Officer who reports into the Global CIO and provides consumer insight and data analytics leadership to the business. The role is responsible for driving the data and digital agenda at corporate level,

but also throughout the organisation. This role owns the group-wide data strategy and works in collaboration with our client-facing parts of the business to deliver products for our clients. This is a critical role to our business.

(Mike Young, CIO, Dentsu Aegis)

Business as usual

One of the most difficult tasks for a new CDO is developing and delivering a data strategy while the organisation continues to operate (and must continue to operate) using and abusing data, continuing with bad habits around data and often with a lack of governance and planning. This has been likened to performing open heart surgery on a runner while they are in the middle of a marathon; they still have to run and compete and finish the race. In reality what has probably been happening is more like patching up the runner, putting a sticking plaster on the heart problem, giving them water to keep them going without a clear map to get them to the end of the race. In most situations for a new CDO the organisation probably feels that it has been operating quite happily without this new person for a very long while – or this will almost certainly be the case in parts of the business and helps to explain low levels of data maturity; people really don't understand the problems that they have. So, for the new CDO it may feel like they are sitting in the corner, talking to themselves. Alternatively, the CDO may be met with comments like 'Yes, we tried that before and it didn't work' or 'IT/Finance/Procurement/ Marketing (delete as appropriate) won't like you doing that', or, our personal favourite, 'That's not how we do that here'.

What is the context of BAU? In most cases (unless the organisation is a start-up) it will be:

- a legacy data environment: silos of data, multiple records, 'duplicates', weak data governance, no useful metadata, no master data management, heavy management information and no business intelligence
- legacy systems: burning platforms (the crisis that means you have to change), bespoke developments, hard to maintain and manage,

reporting systems remote from end-users, no true data
management systems
- legacy business processes: evolved over time, limited by
technology and data available at the point in time, containing
many work-arounds and too dependent on end-user-compute
(EUC) and spreadsheets
- multiple suppliers: of software and systems
- legacy IT department: focused on building 'stuff' rather than
delivering and supporting software-as-a-service, internal networks
as opposed to cloud; perhaps even a 'distant' IT managed service
partner that may be operating to a traditional IT contract with
little time for 'data'
- legacy 'transformation' process: based on project governance and
waterfall, struggling with agile development and innovation or
the more useful blend of the two; not able to adapt to
transformation being data driven rather than technology driven.

But the business will be operating, it will have targets to achieve and
people will be busy running the business. BAU may also consist of
'throwing bodies at the problem', which often makes it hard to get a
clear picture of the business processes and certainly isn't scalable.

A number of these points overlap and it is worth digging a little
deeper to understand the BAU context, and some of this will be very
recognisable. The most immediate 'data threat', or risk, lies in ongoing
projects or programmes within the business. It is very likely that within
the existing project life cycle or within the existing project governance
there is a lack of data design authority. Indeed, any technical design
authority, or solution architecting, may be completely lacking valid data
expertise. Why would the expertise exist if no one really 'owns' the
data? The business will be data users, but the pseudo-ownership will
fall to IT in the absence of anyone else. In fact, at a recent Data Forum
with representatives from both the business and IT sides of
organisations, when the question was posed as to who should take
ownership of data in the absence of a CDO or data functionary, an IT
manager was heard to say, 'IT of course, because the business are idiots'.
We have also heard a Chief Technology Officer say 'Well I own the
CRM', in answer to the question 'Who owns the customer data?'

It is worth making a review of recently delivered or closed projects. A close look at the project documentation, at the outcomes and business value delivered and any actions that were passed into BAU at the end of the project will quickly provide an assessment of the maturity of the data influence in the existing project governance and framework. Often the tell-tale signs of poor data influence are that little consideration was given to data migration until the later stages of a project, there was a lack of discussion about extraction – transformation and loading of data – and a lack of evidence of proper data tooling involved in the project. Perhaps the biggest giveaway is the lack of data governance in the project.

One of the tell-tales of a dysfunctional change process in the portfolio is too many projects starting with assessing the 'as is'. The 'as is' should be artefacts that the business already has and maintains. It is a lot cheaper and easier to set out on a journey if you have a map that already exists and is guaranteed to be up to date. It is a lot more expensive and takes more time if you have to discover and draw your own map every time you wish to start a journey . . . And who builds a new road and doesn't update the map?

It is also interesting to understand who (which function) is currently making the decisions about data in the project: is it someone in IT, is it the technical design authority, is it a project manager or a business analyst, or is it the systems/application owners who are affected by the project?

Existing processes

One of the biggest tasks for the new CDO is the step into this project process and taking control of the data. This will require good communications and a huge amount of credibility, especially if senior sponsorship for the CDO is not visible at this level of detail or if the senior sponsorship doesn't understand this level of detail.

It isn't all doom and gloom. The business, and IT and/or the change delivery function, may realise that projects are struggling because of the lack of good data influence. If this is the case, take the opportunity to bring good data practice to bear as quickly as possible and prove its value to delivering good project outcomes. Work with them, as they may have been trying desperately to do their best in their own areas but were struggling, as it wasn't a joined-up approach. In some cases it will be too late, and projects delivered in the recent history of the business, before the arrival of the CDO, will be leaving a vapour trail of data issues. These need to be picked up and data governance and data quality quickly addressed. Start where the pain is and where the business value is the greatest.

Several of these issues also overlap in the reporting and analytics environment. An immature data environment will reveal inefficient reporting, manifested by too many people in the organisation being involved in extracting, manipulating and pushing data together from disparate sources for the purposes of reporting. There will be duplication of activity, duplication of data sets and a lack of standardised and common reporting methodology and tooling. Again, there will be tell-tale signs for the new CDO to look out for: excessive use of spreadsheets and small databases and multiple small groups across the organisation handling data and reporting activities independently and in silos. To evidence the spreadsheet and database usage, and reveal this to the business and senior sponsors, the new CDO could commission a scan of the organisation's network and look at the amount of storage that is dedicated to various application types. There are many great examples of where a scan of this nature has revealed the immature nature of the data environment. An example which is easy to highlight is the amount of replication that exists in your data landscape: how many times is the same document being stored by different people across your company in different places?

To focus the attention of senior sponsors on the current state of the data nation, it may be worth carrying out a further piece of research and review to establish an estimate of the amount of full-time-equivalent staff time which is expended on reporting, and the number of reports produced. There have been examples of where an organisation is spending more than £4,000 per report for reports of dubious business value. This becomes a strong business case for the CDO to tackle a rationalisation of reporting and data management for reporting, without even getting into the data quality issues which will be present. It is easier to make a financial business case than a data quality business case, but you can solve both problems simultaneously.

Immediate data strategy

The task for the new CDO is how to steer their way through this bubbling cauldron and deliver a data strategy. One approach is to break the task down into two parts: first, an immediate data strategy (IDS), a tactical approach to deliver support for BAU, gain quick wins and temporary fixes and prepare the way for the second part. The additional benefit of the IDS is the delivery of incremental value to the organisation through its data, avoiding the hype cycle on the way. Second is the target data strategy (TDS), the strategic approach. The new CDO cannot sit back and deliver the TDS over a two-to-three-year window; the organisation will probably be expecting some results now, so it is just as important to set realistic expectations as it is to provide some tactical delivery through the IDS. One piece of advice: don't call these tactical deliveries 'projects'. Instead, refer to them as 'initiatives'. This might engender a more agile approach: projects make people think of Gantt charts and lots of time and resources spent on project management.

The IDS should listen to the organisation's data pain and try to deliver high-profile quick wins. The tactical initiatives of the IDS should blend into the strategy of the TDS, and not run down a rabbit hole or blind alley. The IDS should help to build up the narrative and vision of the TDS. The six key elements of the IDS could be:

1   stability and rationalisation of the existing data environment
2   data culture and governance
3   the existing and immediate data and IT development initiatives
4   data exploitation and integration, getting value from the data assets and finding ways to deliver frictionless integration
5   data performance, quality, integrity, assurance and provenance
6   data security (especially with GDPR in mind).

Target data strategy

While the new CDO is delivering the IDS they should be pushing the TDS through business engagement; the organisation needs to be prepared, be ready and believe in the changes that are coming. The CDO should also be using the IDS to show the 'art of the possible' to a data-illiterate business to help the business engage with the new data possibilities. Through the IDS they should be running proof of concepts, feasibility studies, data science initiatives and building a narrative around the vision of the TDS for all levels of the business.

At this point you may want to change your language, depending on what fits, so it could be that, rather than a data strategy, you move towards an information strategy, focusing much more on the value side and what you are using the data for, while still encompassing the data strategy elements. Here you can look at what your information vision is and the principles that underpin it while also looking at how you will deliver this. If your company isn't quite ready for this yet, start with a data strategy and then grow it.

For either strategy, make sure that you:

- use internal communications to sell the vision; don't allow a vacuum to form
- seek every opportunity to communicate the vision; do not be frightened of becoming a data bore, think cheerleader instead
- socialise the data vision and the changes that could be coming, especially the controversial ideas; locate the data champions to support you
- engage the organisation's leadership and find your senior sponsors; they will be crucial
- explain it; if you can't explain it, you're doing something wrong – 'it's me not you'
- win hearts and minds; often a logical argument or business case is not enough to win the day; use your storytelling ability to the maximum.

Casting these six tips in a more practical light, what could a CDO practically do? It may be worth establishing a SWAT (special weapons and tactics) team to address the IDS. The words in SWAT actually sum it up very well. The weapons used, the data tooling, may not be the tools that make up the more strategic data arsenal, and the approach used will be very tactical and not strategic. For example, the CDO may select what might be called 'lightweight tools' for addressing Extract, Transform and Load processes, data storage and data quality. These may be software-as-a-service tools and cloud-based storage to reduce the dependency on IT resources and to operate in a more agile environment and approach. If you have the resources, you can operate two teams: a SWAT team to focus on the IDS and a more transformational team to deliver the TDS, with the CDO maintaining strategic alignment between the two.

Remember, you cannot stop the bus and take the wheels off; the bus has to keep running while you make your changes. It is often difficult to explain to stakeholders that it is possible to build the data foundations while also delivering some of the more advanced data aspirations in data analytics and data science. This is where the communications strategy is important, and raising the data literacy of the stakeholders so that they understand the challenges and how they can be solved. For more detail on this see Chapter 19.

7
Avoiding the hype cycle

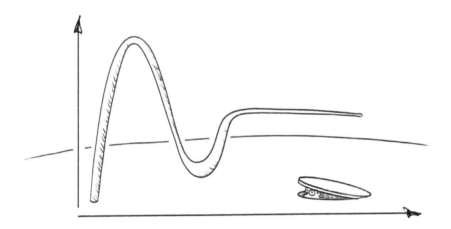

Introduction

This chapter is about managing expectations and describing the features of the Gartner hype cycle. It also explores an approach to the DIKW (Data - Information - Knowledge - Wisdom) pyramid and how to deliver early incremental value to the business in a strategic context.

The Trough of Disillusionment

We have previously talked about the issue of the 'hype cycle' when discussing the ability of the new CDO to shift between the tactical and the strategic. The hype cycle is a Gartner tool to represent the maturity, adoption and social application of specific technologies. It claims to provide a graphical and conceptual presentation of the maturity of emerging technologies through five phases: technology trigger, peak of inflated expectations, trough of disillusionment, slope of enlightenment, plateau of productivity. It has been criticised, not least for not being a cycle:

> The Gartner hype cycle has been criticised for a lack of evidence that it holds, and for not matching well with technological uptake in practice.
>
> (Wikipedia, March 2020)

However, the idea can also help us to understand the challenges facing a new CDO, and to frame the first 100 days and beyond.

Currently, the CDO role is relatively new in many organisations, and, even if it is not, the CDO will arrive into an atmosphere of great expectation. There will be common sentiments that will greet you: 'the business will be transformed into a data-driven business, an organisation capable of making better and more informed decisions based on data; data science will bring the business better insight into its customers and operations; the new CDO will bring big data'. The organisation's data risks, on the enterprise risk register, may even list the arrival of the new CDO as the mitigation.

There will be great expectations about the arrival of the CDO; there will also, in most cases, be a lot of goodwill and enthusiasm in the business for data success. One of the biggest threats to you - certainly in the first 24 months or first 1½ financial years - is the Trough of Disillusionment in the hype cycle. Figure 7.1 shows the features of the

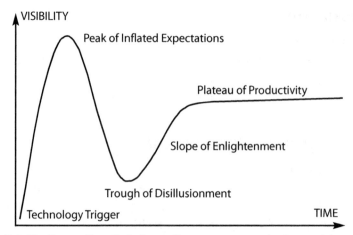

Figure 7.1 *The Gartner Hype Cycle* (https://www.gartner.com/en/research/ methodologies/gartner-hype-cycle). Image sourced from https:// coriniumintelligence.com/chief-data-officer-avoiding-the-hype-cycle.

hype cycle (after Gartner Inc.). The need for the CDO is the Technology Trigger. Expectations rise as soon as the post is advertised and continue to rise once the CDO is in post and during the first few months. Inevitably, unless the expectations are managed, the organisation's hopes will fall into a Trough of Disillusionment if improvements in data are not delivered quickly and if the organisation is not evolving into a data-driven business fast enough. Whether or not the Trough is hit, the organisation will go through a period of enlightenment, either through managing expectations or by education, once it is clear that expectations are not being met. In an ideal world there will be incremental improvement over time.

Data is a new profession at C-Suite level; colleagues, the board or the business may be expecting quick results from the new, data-driven world. You must navigate their way around this hype. If you do this successfully, then you will maintain credibility and sustain the all-important good relationships across the business. So, what tool sets are required to avoid the hype cycle?

As mentioned previously, excellent communication is a good starting point. You must communicate the vision and strategy effectively across the organisation. This communication will be critical to managing the expectations and timescale of the delivery while you are developing the data strategy. The incremental value-adds are the separate battles; while winning the battles is always helpful, what you want is to win the war. Keep your eye on the prize and use your storytelling to describe the journey you are taking people on, making sure that realism sits well embedded within the story.

The second tool for avoiding the hype cycle is incremental value-add. Often, a data strategy can be delivered as separate projects, or as initiatives within the overall programme. We have found that, often, pilot projects, feasibility studies or initiatives can not only add value to the business by fixing an immediate issue but can also show the business the art of the possible, helping to avoid the hype cycle. Alternatively, early delivery of a data governance framework or a piece of advanced analytics providing new insight can also be very effective.

Taking a little time to plan a range of tactical deliveries that fit within the total strategic direction makes sure that as little effort as possible is wasted. Helping the business to understand this can also make sure that you avoid the hype cycle. In the absence of information, people will create their own understandings; giving information is always better than a vacuum. It doesn't have to be in minute detail, but it should be consistent with what you have said before, or come with a good reason for any changes.

In the first edition of this book, and at subsequent presentations and seminars in the intervening two years, we have talked about two things in relation to the hype-cycle challenges facing a new CDO. The first is the need to get the Peak of Expectations under control as soon as possible; the expectations of the senior stakeholders and the business must be set level as quickly as possible. One way of doing this is by carrying out a data maturity assessment, which will open up the conversation and provide some empirical points for discussion. As discussed in an earlier chapter, the data maturity assessment will provide a baseline for setting expectations. It is then up to you to set the expectations as to how fast and how widely you can move from that baseline, and that depends on the existing level of data maturity, the budget available and the desire within all levels of the organisation to shift the data culture. The second challenge is the need to somehow bridge the 'chasm' of the Trough of Disillusionment; somehow, through early wins, incremental delivery and communications you need to leap that gap and move to the Slope of Enlightenment and Plateau of Productivity.

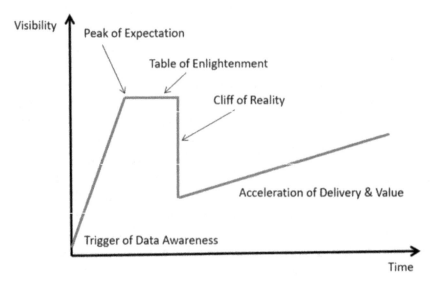

Figure 7.2 *The Carruthers & Jackson CDO journey*

We've learned a lot in the past two years, and although we still believe that those two pieces of advice (get expectations under control and bridge the trough) still hold good, we have recast the hype cycle into a new model for CDOs 'The Carruthers & Jackson CDO journey'.

The Trigger of Data Awareness

At some point the organisation becomes aware that it needs a CDO, or a senior data leader, to be responsible and accountable for the organisation's data and for deriving value from it. We identify several things that may trigger this awareness: regulatory pressures, commercial pressures and opportunities, operational pressures and opportunities, the potential for customer delight and simply because everyone else is getting one! At this point the organisation decides to recruit a CDO.

Peak of Expectations

We have already discussed that almost as soon as the Trigger of Data Awareness has been pulled, expectations will begin to mount.

Table of Enlightenment

We now realise that the CDO needs to harness these expectations and turn them to their advantage. Take the senior stakeholders and the business on a journey of enlightenment, educate them, but do this without squashing or deflating their expectations. Use their expectations to secure budget and set an agenda and strategy. The education process and raising of data literacy will bring the stakeholder to the edge of the Table of Enlightenment.

Cliff of Reality

If data education and improvement in data literacy have been successful, perhaps supported by a data maturity assessment, your stakeholders will descend the Cliff of Reality, they will reset their own and the organisation's expectations. They will realise the task and challenges, and the journey, that are faced by the whole organisation, and not just the CDO, to become data mature.

Acceleration of Delivery and Value

At the foot of the Cliff of Reality, the Acceleration of Delivery and Value can begin.

Data to wisdom

It is accepted that wisdom is built on knowledge, and knowledge is underpinned by information, and that data is the building block of information. The DIKW (Data/Information/Knowledge/Wisdom) pyramid (Figure 7.3) is a useful tool for understanding and communicating an approach to avoiding the hype cycle. While common sense, and the DIKW pyramid, tells every CDO, and every board member, that the strategic approach starts by getting the data foundations firm and stable (otherwise the pyramid will fall down), expectations and the Trough of Disillusionment, or the Table of Enlightenment, have to be managed. In our book *Data Driven Business Transformation* we have changed the terminology use in the second layer of the pyramid from 'Information' to 'Collected, Curated and Contextualised Data' (CCC Data). We have done this for three reasons: first, the term 'information' causes too much confusion in organisations, for example with the role of the CIO or Information Architecture;

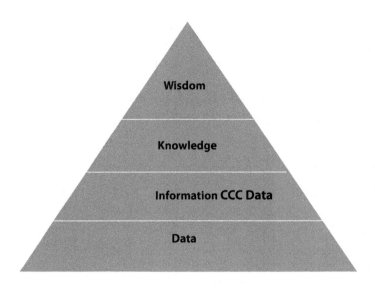

Figure 7.3 *The DIKW pyramid*

second, because this is really what information is - collected, curated and contextualised data; and third, the term CCC Data describes really well what needs to be done to data to derive value from the raw data.

The only problem with this diagram is that it suggests that this is a linear process, and data is anything but linear. While the basic understanding of this triangle is accurate, just remember that you will have various iterations moving around in the triangle, rather than resolving all your data problems and then tackling your information, and then knowledge, to arrive at wisdom.

If you hold off from delivering almost immediate incremental value, or fail to tackle the burning platforms because you are concentrating on fixing the foundations, then you can understand why disillusion may set in with the CEO, board and colleagues, however much you tell them about the strategic approach.

To avoid this peril, and to address the burning platforms that may be putting the business at risk, you should strike vertically up the DIKW pyramid in a small segment or use case. So, find somewhere, a small pocket of activity or discrete part of the business, where there is either 'data opportunity' or something that can and needs to be fixed fast, or real insight that could be delivered from analytics. Pick this area, fix the data layer that underpins it as best you can, using the right tooling, bring this data together to create assured and valued information for the business; then have the conversation with the business about the knowledge and wisdom that can be derived and brought to real business advantage.

This vertical strike, because it is part of the pyramid, though tactical, will be part of the final construction, and so will add to the whole of the strategic landscape you are creating. In this way the pyramid is simultaneously being built horizontally and vertically. Therefore the pyramid may get built more quickly and you get the opportunity to deliver incremental value.

The real trick is in selecting the order of the vertical strikes; it is clearly best if they are 'close' to each other, rather than standing as lone pillars. Figure 7.4 on the next page illustrates this. The closer they are, the more strategic they can be and the stronger they will build. It might also mean that you can justify funding, as it takes less time to build onto something rather than constantly starting from scratch.

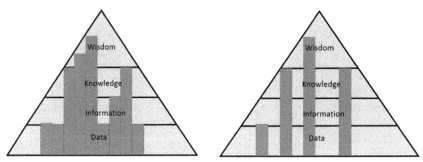

Figure 7.4 *Strong, aligned vertical strikes versus weak, disjointed ones*

The vertical striking approach has the benefit of quickly demonstrating to the business the 'art of the possible' and providing the opportunity to be an evangelist for new ways of working and/or technologies. It also de-risks, to a great extent, the whole process of building the pyramid. We have found that this process is a very good way to engage with the companies you bring in to help, both suppliers and consultancies, and run these strikes as proof of concepts (PoC) or demonstrations of business value. Most vendors leap at the opportunity to show the power, flexibility and benefit of their systems, which is great, as long as you remember the business side of things too.

If these strikes are delivered as part of a PoC, the CDO should have one eye firmly fixed on how to operationalise it quickly. If the PoC really does prove value to the business, the business will not want to let it stand down. If you can't achieve this, then you may have avoided the initial Trough of Disillusionment only to walk into a second trough that has followed close behind. We are becoming increasingly convinced that a minimal viable product is of more value and quicker to move into delivering value than a PoC or proof of value (PoV). Let's not waste any effort that we don't need to!

Remember to use that great team you brought in to help you. Throughout this process, as well as working on your vertical strikes with your SWAT team you need to manage the expectations of the business; interacting with suppliers is a big task and the CDO will need support. So having the support of a strong number two, project managers, business analysts and the business will be essential.

So, what are the two things that need to be focused on while the vertical strikes are mobilising?

First, communicate the plan of these strikes to the leadership team so that they understand clearly what is going on and their expectations are managed, and so that they understand the scaling implications if that is the outcome. Leadership teams don't like shocks: manage them way ahead of time. It is important to build a 'narrative' around these 'tactical vertical strikes' or PoCs. Build a story that is recognisable across the business and uses a common language, so that the whole business is buying in to the same thing and outcomes. These early vertical strikes do provide the opportunity for the CDO's team to create and propagate the common language of 'data' that will be used in the business. For example, if one of these strikes is a data extraction, transformation and load (ETL) exercise, doing away with inefficient legacy work around processes involving spreadsheets, the whole business will soon start using terms like ETL and understanding that this is a 'data process' and how it fits into other projects and business processes.

One vertical strike may be to deliver some advanced analytics, provide some insight on behaviours or provide the ability to predict future events. It may be possible to wrangle good data, work it through sound analytics and provide some insight. This sort of vertical strike has many benefits. First, being a vertical strike, it is contained and shouldn't take forever; second, it demonstrates the art of the possible and helps the business 'see' what it is getting; third, it draws 'data' people across an organisation together, because they may be interested to understand and be involved in what is going on; and last, it should provide some valuable business insight which could be operationalised.

Use the process and outcomes as part of your data story to capture the interest of senior colleagues and the board. As the storyteller, you need to interpret through a story what the data has revealed. The story is very like a parable:

> A simple story used to illustrate a data lesson.
> (Google Dictionary, definition adapted for purpose)

Next, focus on the strategic vision, and never lose sight of the vision of the completed pyramid. It can be very easy to get drawn into the here and now, the tactical, and lose focus on the strategic. Keep delivering the strategic narrative to the board and colleagues and throughout the business, and keep building those relationships with Finance, Procurement, HR and IT in order to deliver it.

The rest of the hype cycle

It is worth being aware of the other features of the hype cycle in case this is the uncontrolled route that your journey takes if you can't shift the journey into the Carruthers & Jackson CDO Journey. Apart from the Trough of Disillusionment the hype cycle has three other features to be aware of and to take care to manage. The first is the Peak of Inflated Expectations. The clue is in the name: don't allow the expectations of the organisation, colleagues or the board to become inflated. Manage these expectations so that they are realistic and achievable, and be very clear about the dependencies of these expectations – which may be resources, budget, capability, IT and change delivery resources and/or the timescales for procurement. The factors beyond your control are almost endless, but if you understand them you can use them in the story you create to manage expectations. Just having a 'strategy', a great vision on paper or in a slide deck, does not get problems solved.

Second, the Plateau of Productivity should be very carefully managed. Manage the gradient of the rise to the Plateau so that it isn't too steep and sudden. It's better that 'data' has a gradual, strong growth in visibility within the business rather than a sudden dash to the Plateau that may be hard to maintain. If the growth in data visibility is more prolonged it may extend over more financial accounting periods, thereby providing data with access to more funds to deliver change. It is also true that any organisation can only cope with so much change at a time. A sudden rise in data developments, projects and delivery may be overwhelming for an organisation, which can result in new techniques, approaches and technology not being delivered effectively.

The hype cycle is an opportunity as well as a danger. Avoiding the troughs may not result in a small incremental rise in value-add; the progression may be more stepped. In reality this probably will be the case, so communications around this process need to be flexible. Acknowledging the challenges that exist and having a plan to mitigate them helps you to gain credibility and trust.

8
Relating to the rest of the business, especially the C-Suite

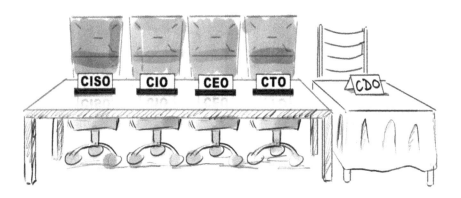

Introduction

This chapter explores the idea that the CDO is different to the Chief Technology Officer (CTO) or Chief Information Officer (CIO) and discusses the relationship that the CDO might have with the Chief Executive Officer (CEO). The key role of the CDO and data ownership is examined. This chapter is aimed at the business stakeholders.

There are more C-Suite roles than there used to be. The long-established roles of Chief Executive and Chief Information Officer now have to compete for room at the table with roles like the Chief Information Security Officer, Chief Operating Officer, Chief Finance Officer, Chief Customer Officer, Chief Digital Officer and, of course, the Chief Data Officer – it's getting a bit crowded around the table.

Key relationships

Relationship building is a key skill for the CDO. Working with the data means you, the CDO, are cutting across the silos in the organisation and therefore potentially messing around in everyone's backyard, so you had better be able to ask nicely before you do, or have some air cover for when an area feels pain for the greater good! While the CDO needs to form a working relationship with any other stakeholders in the company, not just the rest of the C-Suite, the one that causes the most concern is the relationship with CIO or CTO; it definitely generates the most questions at conferences. Of course these roles and their scope vary from organisation to organisation.

The difference between a CIO and CDO (apart from the words 'information' and 'data') is best described using the bucket-and-water analogy. The CIO is responsible for the bucket (the technology), ensuring that it is complete, without any holes in it, that the bucket is the right size, with just a little bit of spare room but not too much and it's all in a safe place. The CDO is responsible for the liquid (the data) you put in the bucket, ensuring that it is the right liquid, the right amount, and that it is not contaminated. The CDO is also responsible for what happens to the liquid; making it available when it's needed. In this analogy the CIO has a responsibility to make the water accessible to the CDO (the business). In this respect the CIO has competing demands: on the one hand, to keep the water safe and secure to make sure that no one steals it or contaminates it, and on the other hand to make sure that the business can access the water easily, otherwise they will die of thirst. Too often the first use case takes priority and the second is neglected, which stifles the organisation's potential to derive value from its data.

If the organisation has a CIO who is responsible for both, then it is doing great and probably doesn't need a CDO as well; however, it's a really big expectation to cover both roles, which often require two very different skill and experience sets. In the past, lots of organisations assumed the CIO was doing both, while the CIO assumed that the business was accountable for the data – hence leading to some of the problems we are facing now. Just remember what happens when you assume anything! It may also be the case that the CIO role isn't so much focused on deriving insight and value from the data, or from deriving innovation from the data. To get both roles they need a very symbiotic relationship where there is a healthy respect for each role.

The other role that it's important for the CDO to relate to is the CEO. By tucking the CDO role under other roles like the CIO it becomes tangled up with the technology. This just confuses the business, which has a hard enough time sorting through the difference between looking after the data and information and looking after the tools you use to look after the data and information. Why make it more complicated for them? Where the business places the CDO also demonstrates to the rest of the organisation how much it values its data. Placing the role so far from the CEO that one can see too much daylight between the CEO and CDO isn't really telling anyone that the business values its data. However, we're not suggesting that the CDO is the most important role in the organisation, either – just that a balance needs to be struck that works for the organisation. We also reflect on the fact that Gartner predicts a good percentage of CDOs will fail, and one of the causes of this failure is attributable to the CDO's being too far away from the rest of the C-Suite, too junior.

If getting value is high on the organisation's agenda, then that should be reflected in where the CDO role is placed, as it helps with the CDO's reach across the business. If the major focus is risk-averse, then perhaps the organisation's governance or technical authority function is the right place.

If there is a Chief Analytics Officer (CAO) or Chief Unicorn (that key element of your data science team that equally understands the technology, data science and business) then they are going to be another C that the CDO needs to focus on; as CDO, you are feeding them the lifeblood that they need to perform their role, so you become half of a very important double act for the organisation. When you get to the point of finishing each other's sentences, then you might be just about close enough! This is why the analytics or data science role fits well into the remit of the CDO. If they are put together, giving the CDO the responsibility and accountability not only to look after the data but also to derive value and insight from the data, then you can see that it is quite a large remit and worthy of that senior role and position in the organisation.

Other interesting relationships that you will build are with the Finance, HR and Procurement departments. While the analytical side of the company will probably be focused externally and making the big decisions, the Finance and HR departments are crucial to how the company runs: don't underestimate the time you will need to spend with them. Whereas you are more of a feeder for a CAO, you have a two-way flow with the Finance and HR functions, with constant ebb and flow back and forth. It is always more complicated when you are both a customer and a supplier in a relationship, but building the relationship with respect, trust and all the other skills we talked about in Chapter 4 will come into play heavily here. We believe that it is also worth sharing your plan and visions with these teams, as they will be key partners in supporting your team recruitment, reskilling, onboarding new data technology and establishing your budget. Also, Finance and HR often are just as desperate for help to 'fix' data problems which they face.

You will be heavily reliant on your Chief Information Security Officer (CISO). This tends to be one of those C roles that aren't operating at director level. With the current changing landscape around cyber-attacks spilling over into what looks like grand-scale, worldwide attacks, wherever the CISO is placed in your organisation, don't ignore them. In the same way that you are advising the organisation on all things data, your CISO is the specialist that you might reason with occasionally when they get a bit purist, but you must always listen to.

The other CDO, in many cases will also be an important partner. The other CDO – yes, the Chief Digital Officer, the person who is driving the organisation's digital development and online customer interaction. This CDO is a key partner, they will rely on good data, supplied at pace and with resilience, while at that same time their platforms will be collecting and harvesting data that will be important for your vision.

The introduction of GDPR has made one other relationship outside the C-Suite of rising importance to the CDO. This is the relationship with the Data Protection Officer (DPO). Both the DPO and the CDO may be new to an organisation, so there is perhaps the double whammy of two previously unknown roles at the table who at the same time will be trying to work out their own new working relationships. However, both being 'data' professionals and understanding the value and importance of data, they should be close allies and a strong and consistent voice to their C-Suite colleagues.

So, in a nutshell, relationship building is a key part of being a CDO – but we think we might have already mentioned that.

Building a relationship is a bit like a dance: there has to be give and take, but someone has to make the first move. We've always found that everyone is interesting and has something unique that makes them special. Getting to know them gives you an opportunity to find out what that is. Don't expect to have a fantastic relationship overnight – these things do take time; but the bit which a lot of people forget is that they also take effort. Make sure that you do set up meetings when you say you will, and do what you say you will do. Trust is such an important element of any relationship and it takes time to build, but only seconds to destroy.

The thing that it is probably worth stressing here – and this is relevant to the entire content of this book – is that all of this must be tailored to the organisation you work with. There is no silver bullet or magic silhouette that will automatically 'fix' a company. There isn't a set process that, if you follow it to the letter, will lead you to data nirvana. What there is, is a set of tools to use that will give you a way forward. So much of what you will be dealing with will depend on the legacy state of the business, the type of organisation you are in, what culture you are dealing with, what has come on the data path before you. Keep agile and flexible, using all the tools but always thinking about what you are trying to achieve and pulling the right tool from the bag, rather than following a prescriptive procedure. No process has been invented that can cover every eventuality, and one thing that we have learned is that you have never seen it all – there is always that one situation that you end up looking at with your head tilted, thinking 'But how did that even happen?'

> I was previously in business compliance and data security, and as Chief Data Officer my priorities are security and privacy of data. I work with heads of security and privacy officers for seven counties so we know where our data is. I'm in the middle as CDO, the spider making sure our data is taken care of.
>
> (Vanessa Eriksson, Chief Data Officer, TeliaSonera)

Relating to the rest of the C-Suite – well, the CDO has to be their friend and educator. Hopefully, at some point in the future this won't be so needed, but certainly now the CDO has to help the rest of the senior leaders with their data literacy. The CDO needs to help, support and facilitate improvement in data literacy across the C-Suite. It is quite probable that senior colleagues will have risen to their leadership roles as subject matter experts in their fields, with huge amounts of business acumen and experience, huge amounts of leadership and strategy skills and vision, but very little in terms of a background in data. Even the most numerate of colleagues – and there are a lot in financial services – will not understand or appreciate data governance, metadata, modern data tooling, DataOps or data architecture. The CDO will also need to persuade senior colleagues to take executive ownership for the data in their domains. So, if you can, increase the data literacy of your senior colleagues and get them to buy in to data ownership. It is worth remembering that an organisation that is starting from a low level of data maturity will probably have very little data governance or data ownership. Therefore, introducing a little of both, especially focused on the critical data elements, has the potential to make a big impact. Data governance will improve data quality and reduce data friction. Knowing your data, making your data transparent to the business, having data owners and data stewards to monitor and look after the data, and who call out when their data isn't 'right', will improve data quality and reduce the frictions. A small step at a low level of data maturity can have disproportionately large beneficial impacts. It also engages the business and shows them what is ahead.

9
The Chief Data Officer as a disruptor

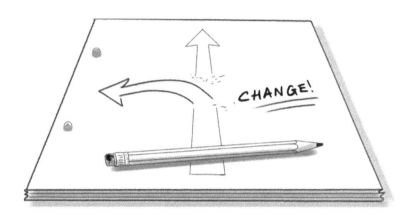

Introduction

This chapter explores the concept of disruption and what it means, and whether the CDO is a disruptor or an innovator. The role of data as a disruptor is examined.

Without a doubt, many parts of a business may find a CDO challenging as they suggest different and better ways of doing things, especially related to data.

Disruption and innovation

Disruption: to radically change an industry, business strategy, etc.

(www.dictionary.com)

If this is the definition, then we don't really think that in most cases the CDO is a disruptor, or indeed should be a disruptor. If you are a first-generation CDO (FCDO, probably the first CDO the business has seen) then you are probably risk-averse (more about this in Chapter 12, which explores the different generations of the CDO). In data terms, the business is probably in a fragile state – certainly in a state where the first imperative is to stabilise the current position and put out the burning fires. There is too much at stake in the early days for the FCDO to be a disruptor.

However, there is often confusion between disruption and innovation:

> People are sometimes confused about the difference between innovation and disruption. It's not exactly black and white, but there are real distinctions, and it's not just splitting hairs. Think of it this way: Disruptors are innovators, but not all innovators are disruptors – in the same way that a square is a rectangle but not all rectangles are squares. Still with me?
>
> Innovation and disruption are similar in that they are both makers and builders. Disruption takes a left turn by literally uprooting and changing how we think, behave, do business, learn and go about our day-to-day.
> (Caroline Howard, Forbes Staff 'Disruption v Innovation: What's the difference?' *Forbes*, March 2013)

Innovation, then, introduces new ways of doing things but maintains the same course and doesn't suggest a left turn. The majority of the products and services of the organisation, or its purpose, remain the same, they are just done in new ways. The FCDO is probably more of an innovator than a disruptor. The FCDO will suggest new ways of doing things, with new tools, and will transform the business through innovation. The outcome is that business essentially looks the same and does the same thing, with largely the same group of people; it just does it in a slightly different way. Innovation is a leap forward, perhaps for organisations which are 'lagging' behind the 'wave' and are just followers of others. Innovation suggests leapfrogging others (perhaps using their experience and mistakes) and getting close to the top of the wave, or even its leading edge.

Innovation is crucial to the continuing success of any organisation.

The fundamental key to any data strategy is its complete alignment to delivering the business objectives. Therefore an FCDO cannot be a disruptor, unless the business objective is to disrupt from within. The data strategy, if aligned to the business objectives, cannot propose a left turn. However, it is clear that the data strategy may propose innovative ways of achieving the business objectives, and it is more than probable that the CDO, through the data strategy, will suggest innovative ways of delivering them.

The professional services firm EY currently identifies four technology areas that it believes are key to innovation: Artificial Intelligence (AI), Robotic Process Automation (RPA), Blockchain and Analytics. At least three of these are pure 'data', therefore it would be impossible for an effective FCDO *not* to be an innovator. The fourth, RPA, is increasingly coming into the realm of data through data automation and straight-through processing. The data approach to automation will focus on reshaping the business process around the data rather than using RPA to automate what in many cases is a broken business process.

How CDOs may innovate and disrupt

We don't think that a CEO would allow an FCDO to be a disruptor; the risk would be too great. The CEO needs to maintain the right balance between risk and innovation. However, we have suggested that the second-generation CDO (SCDO) may well be a disruptor. The SCDO is coming into a data environment that is more stable, the data quality is good and the data is mastered, governed and handled in the right way, and it is valued. This environment would allow an SCDO to be disruptive, to suggest the left turns.

> Insights generated by big data can result in considerable optimisations for a company. However, tomorrow's technological innovations have a much greater potential. Data Analytics can bring down established business models. Opportunities abound for anyone who is aware of the possible impact.
>
> (Jo Coutuer, Deloitte, March 2015)

The SCDO who brings value-add, probably through data analytics, has the potential to bring down the established business model, especially if the data analytics are placed at the heart of the business processes and drive the decision-making processes.

Advanced analytics and data science will reveal insight that has not been visible before. Organisations will know their next best action and will cease to be reactive; they will be more proactive in their customer engagement, customer service, asset management and/or asset maintenance. In fact it may be the business that itself becomes the disruptor, once it has the revelations and insights provided by advanced analytics, machine learning and AI.

Both the FCDO and the SCDO will demonstrate 'entrepreneurial behaviour'; they see the potential in an innovation and bring it to bear in the business or marketplace, more often than not managing some level of risk. For the sake of further discussion, now that we are aware of the difference between innovation and disruption, let's take a look at where a CDO may be innovative/disruptive.

The first place is fairly obvious: technology. The CDO will be introducing new 'data technology' to the business, the FCDO may be introducing technology for master data management and metadata, and/or some form of ETL/ELT (extract, transform, load/extract, load, transform) tool and data vault. The FCDO may also be innovating, with new reporting and dashboarding technologies that move way beyond the static spreadsheets with embedded macros. The SCDO may well be introducing new programming languages such as R and Python, which the business has not used before, or indeed machine learning and data science platforms that support the rise of the subject-matter expert citizen data scientist.

The second place is the target operating model (TOM) and organisational design (OD). The FCDO may drive some of the decision-making and operational procedures to change through improved insight gained from actionable data. The FCDO may also affect the OD by creating a data team and centralising some of the data and reporting functions to create a centre of excellence to support the business, as well as by creating standardised methodology and tooling. The SCDO may well have a greater influence on transforming the TOM, through suggesting the left turn. By the time the SCDO is in place, the business leadership should have built up enough trust in 'data' to take the left turn. The operating model will lead to the establishment of a DataOps function to supply data products and services to the business at pace.

This will drive innovation. When the business gets access to trusted data at the pace they require, they will become the drivers of innovation (and even disruption).

The CDOs may influence transformation in the business location, shape and size. As the business makes more effective decisions, more efficiently, it may restructure, change its business location, downsize the workforce and/or relocate some if not all of its functions.

Some innovation or disruption may be in the data itself. Instead of collecting mass data (see Chapter 16), the business may collect less, not more; less data but better data. There may also be value in the data either directly within the business or for sale to other organisations. This new value in data may have a positive effect on the balance sheet – data becomes an asset. It may be the insights derived from the data that can be monetised, rather than raw data. Or the new approach to data may allow the business to develop new revenue streams. Data may even be the driving force behind future mergers and acquisitions. Organisations wishing to get hold of the data asset of another business, just as previously they wanted to get hold of physical assets, cash or customer bases, would consider an acquisition or merger.

Data is the disruptor

> From the dawn of civilisation until 2003, humankind generated 5 exabytes of data. Now we produce 5 exabytes every two days . . . and the pace is accelerating.
>
> (Eric Schmidt, Executive Chairman, Google)

A discussion on the BBC Radio 4's *Today* programme in June 2017 concerned a new report from the UK's science academy, which proposed that urgent consideration needed to be given to the 'careful stewardship' needed over the next ten years to ensure that the dividends from machine learning benefit all in UK society. The discussion really brought out the fact that the disruption that needs to be managed and put into careful stewardship isn't in fact the technology; it is the data and the use of the data. It is significant that the European Union expended a huge amount of time in developing the General Data Protection Regulation. Data is the disruptor, not the

CDO. In August 2019 this was reflected by the UK's Health Secretary, Matt Hancock, announcing an investment of £250m in AI for the NHS.

> My task is to ensure the NHS has the funding it needs to make a real difference to the lives of staff and patients. Transforming care through artificial intelligence is a perfect illustration of that. We are on the cusp of a huge health tech revolution that could transform patient experience by making the NHS a truly predictive, preventive and personalised health and care service.
>
> (Matt Hancock, Secretary of State for Health and Social Care,
> August 2019)

10
Building the Chief Data Officer team

Introduction

This chapter explains why the CDO needs a team, who is needed in that team and the skill sets that are required. The shape and size of the data team are discussed, and the balance in the team between science and arts.

> I felt the need to build a data team quickly to address the immediate data problems and enable me to remain strategic with at least 60% of my head space. Often my first recruits are from existing internal colleagues who understand the business and the existing data issues. I certainly felt the need to get help ASAP from a team, expectations are often high and you can't do it alone ... And it can get lonely, you need some people to share ideas and observations!
>
> (Peter Jackson)

The basics of the team

Let's assume that you have the right support structure in place, such as any administrative or project support roles. We think those roles are pretty well documented, so you probably don't need us to tell you what works for you in that area. Equally, there are already well-documented descriptions of what makes up an information security or data protection team, or what you need in order to focus on records management, so we have focused only on the new roles that complement the CDO area and form the core components of what could be a new team to the organisation.

We know that right now there are different types of CDO, which we have labelled first and second generation (we discuss those again later in the book), but, for now, imagine the first generation is focused on being risk-averse and the second generation is focused on value-add. In this chapter we are talking about what an FCDO needs to form their team and what a generation SCDO needs on top of that structure.

The basics that you need to put in place are the same for both teams. Only you can decide the balance of people you want in each role across the team, but our advice would be to start small, make sure you have coverage of each of the following areas and then grow at a pace that works for your business.

Bear in mind that the FCDO cannot be everywhere all the time; they will want to be, but, more importantly, they will need to get a handle on the business, a handle on the burning platforms, to stop more mistakes from happening, to start changing behaviours and culture and to start spreading the word. They need to be visible . . . and at the same time they need to be managing up and across, they need to keep the data message going to the CEO and the board (the board may expect this anyway) or to fellow directors or other senior colleagues. So, early on, a trusted, data-savvy lieutenant is essential; and quickly backing this up with a team that all works together will help you to keep your sanity.

You obviously need to form some kind of structure to your team, and this will normally mean starting with a relatively small team before you can demonstrate the value of what you can achieve, and then growing the team to the right size. There are certain pillars that you need to have as part of your team. We aren't suggesting that you have to have four structures, or that each of these has to report to you directly, but that these areas do need to be represented within your overall structure. We have heard different labels attached to each of these pillars and roles, but there has not been any quibbling about whether they are needed, and we aren't suggesting that the titles below are the only ones that cover these areas. It is the areas that are important, and these also tie in to the themes within the first 100 days (see Chapter 5). Feel free to call them what you like.

The different pillars

DataOps

DataOps (or Data Operations) works iteratively with the business team to shape, create and deliver sustainable data solutions that meet and exceed the business expectations. At its core it's about aligning the way you manage data with what you want to do with it, with a focus on the practical aspects of how you do that. It focuses on cultivating data practices and processes that improve the speed of analytics, including data access, quality control, automation, integration, as well as model deployment and management. It's a very agile way of doing data and that fits well with the constantly changing nature of data.

This is the area that delivers your compelling visualisations to help you bring data to life and tell that compelling story, making it easier to make data-driven decisions.

Data analysts

Both the data stewards and the data analysts form the part of the team that helps to improve data quality throughout your organisation. On balance, you might need a small number of information architects, but you will need a much higher proportion of stewards and analysts, and they will need to cover a great deal of ground. They are the bulk of your data army.

Data analysts, or business analysts with a data head, work closely with the data stewards, supporting them and learning from them. This is one of the entry-level roles within your team for people who have the right level of curiosity and analytical skills, learning about the business and focused on helping it to understand the detail behind the data and information that it uses and how to improve it. In their own right, data analysts are detailed, and will get really in-depth with the data problems, finding out what are the root causes of the problems by tracing through what might be mega lines of data. Try to balance the mix of what you give these people to do, if for no other reason than for their sanity; no one can spend every day staring at the mother-of-all-spreadsheets without a break. Just make sure that you mix it up and give them the chance to balance their skills development.

Data engineers

The data engineer's role is also important here. Their primary role is to prepare the data to be used by the analytical or data science functions or for the business to get value from it. This is a really varied role but includes pulling data pipelines together from different sources, integrating, consolidating and cleansing data and then structuring it so that it becomes useful.

Data governance

Governance establishes the rules of the game you are playing when it comes to data, and for more on this please look at Chapter 18. Data Governance is such a core area that it has its own chapter. There is no excuse for not getting your basics right when it comes to data, and this is the area that helps you do that.

Governance specialists

In the past, most organisations have tried to control their data, with varying degrees of success, which means that they probably have a policy or two lying around that documents what they want people to do with the company's data. In the case of large, siloed organisations you will very probably have lots of pockets of good(ish) practice around the company where people have tried their best to do the right thing and have created their own standards in the absence of being able to find one. So, typically, when you come in there will be a complex set of policies, standards, procedures and guidelines – call them whatever you want – that govern what people need to do. In most cases the employees are being set up to fail, as these policies have been developed within those silos, they aren't joined up, they sometimes contradict each other, they don't cover everything . . . in other words, it's a mess.

Bringing in a governance specialist to help you sort out this mess can really save you time in the long run. They can help the company to create the structure that explains clearly, simply and concisely what obligations everyone in the company has regarding the treatment of data and what you want them to do about it, as well as helping to define the structure that keeps them all up to date. It is up to you how long you keep this role. Once the mess is sorted out, with a structure in place to keep it up to date, you might choose to absorb the responsibilities into other roles in the team, or you might decide to maintain something in place that keeps a focus on this area; only you will know how much emphasis is needed when the team is in a business-as-usual state.

We might focus on talking about data strategy, which is right as you need to be looking at where you are going most of the time, but this area provides a very important counterbalance – that of understanding, monitoring and mitigating your data risk. Now, when we say mitigating in this context, it isn't that this is the only team doing anything to mitigate the risks; since data is everyone's concern it would be rather unfair to land one team with the whole problem. Instead, it is their role to agree and monitor the action on those mitigations, making sure that the whole machine of your organisation works together well.

Data proposition

This pillar is about defining what the data products or assets are, and the main focus of this area is on delivery – working with the business, understanding what it wants and or needs (as they aren't always the same thing) and figuring out how to get there. What order do you create the products in, what value is there in each product delivery and what is the roadmap to deliver them?

This is the area that looks after what you can view as your business development managers, that works with the rest of the organisation to make sure that you have a steady flow of work; sometimes this is demand generation and sometimes it's being a gatekeeper. It is vitally important to track the value of what the whole team are delivering, in order to demonstrate that value. It isn't enough to deliver brilliant work, it's important that the rest of the organisation know what you are doing, so they want to work with you in a productive way.

Data steward

The data steward is a typical role under this heading.

How many projects have you worked on where you hand someone a piece of paper with the instructions on and they immediately come out of their comfort zone and change their behaviour without any prompting and do exactly what you need them to do? Such events are really few and far between. We're not saying that they're impossible, but we expect we would sooner see a hippopotamus wearing a tutu dancing through Newcastle before we found one. This is where your data stewards come in. They are your data specialists, who know the most about what the organisation *should* be doing with its data and want to help the business get to data nirvana.

Data stewards sit within your teams and are your data cheerleaders; they are your main conduits out to the business areas and should spend a great deal of their time within the business listening to it. If they are sitting at their desks, then you need to ask them what they are doing; otherwise, let them get on and do their job. They are the data and information experts who work heavily with the business to improve the understanding of what its responsibilities are regarding data and information - whether that is by training, investigating root causes of data problems, working on action plans or providing assurance activities. The relationship your data stewards have with the business will be a major part of why your 'hearts and minds' campaign will succeed or fail.

They are carrying out a wonderful, multitasking beast of a role, but first and foremost they are part of your data cheerleading team. They love data as much as you do and can't wait to get out there to help parts of the business get the most from their information. They are experts in data regulations and information best practice, and ninjas in making governance look like fun (or at least, fundamental). We can't stress the value of this role within your team enough.

Data architecture

The data architecture piece works with all the other different variants of architects within your organisation - enterprise, IT, systems - to establish a data landscape which will be driven to supporting the data strategy and, ultimately, the business strategy. It's probably obvious that this is where the information or data architects will be found.

Information architects (data architects)

Have you ever tried to use a library without any kind of indexing system in place? It would be a giant pile of paper, and finding anything would be a case of good fortune. You don't have to: when you use a library you have indexes that help you find what you need, whether you are looking for the latest book by your favourite author or just know that you fancy a new, heart-pumping thriller. The exact same book is catalogued in a myriad of different ways that allow you to find it. However, it doesn't change shelf depending on the path you take; rather, all paths led to the same place.

Now wouldn't it be a good idea if you could treat your data and information in the same way: it stays in the same place but you always end up at the same point, no matter how you look for it? This is where your information architect comes in; they build the structures and frameworks to help you get the best from your data. They understand how your company uses information and turn that into conceptual models, which you can use to understand who is responsible for your information domains and therefore who is really accountable for making decisions about sections of your information. This is the area that eventually gives you your master data management and data models. The data architect understands the data at field level, the physical model, they will understand the data lineage. An application architect will understand the data at an application level, so often they are called system architects; this is the logical model. The enterprise architects understand data at the enterprise level, which is the business process level and is the conceptual model. Many organisations, especially those which have a low level of data maturity, have not had true data architects, so this is an important hire.

Some roles sit outside your structure but are still fundamental to how you work across the organisation.

Information (data) champions

Technically, the champions don't sit within your team but work closely with it. They normally have full-time jobs in different business areas and are experts and influential in those areas. They don't need to be data experts but, rather, enthusiastic amateurs who will work with your team (especially the data stewards) to help your understanding of what their business area needs and help the business area to improve its maturity regarding data and information management.

You should recognise that it's incredibly hard for these people, as they will in all likelihood have a full-time job to do which doesn't include the extra that you need them to do. If they are good (and let's face it, the good ones are the ones you want), they will already be busy. They may be volunteers, but possibly not willing ones, as the press-gang mentality is still alive and well in corporations, so they are your first engagement challenge. Work with them to understand their area, find out why it is important for them, what data can do *for them*. Nurture these people, and the time and effort you put in will be rewarded tenfold. The data stewards and the information champions are the main 'face' that the company sees when looking at good data management; make it a positive one.

Project managers

This is not strictly a data role but is completely necessary, all the same. You will be working often with a matrix team and you will need the skills of a good project manager to keep your vision and strategy on track. In fact, while we are on the subject, it's worth mentioning that there are a number of IT and business roles that you don't need to muck around with – they already exist. You will need to work with enterprise and solution architects, with financial specialists and with various other roles that are already well established. You have enough on your plate, so don't reinvent the wheel; grabbing someone from another department and sticking data or information in the job title doesn't make it a specialist role. If the role already exists and is doing what you need it to do, then leave it alone; step away from the empire-building trap and focus on what you do need to do.

Information (data) asset owners

Tying in to the work of the information architect, information asset owners are the people who are responsible for looking after the different information (data) domains; they are accountable for making decisions about particular defined areas and are experts in their fields. While they don't sit as part of your core team, that doesn't make them any less critical to have working with you.

Centralised or dispersed?

Building the CDO team will also heavily depend on the context. Without a doubt the close team in the 'CDO office' may have a lot of commonality. Beyond that close group the team may vary in structure or shape. There are two common scenarios. First, the organisation is quite 'data mature' in terms of its data management and reporting, or it may be very geographically dispersed, in which case a hub-and-spoke structure may be appropriate – a central hub of the CDO office and a small group of data SME (subject matter expertise) with data functions dispersed across the organisation. This is a democratised approach and may be the optimum structure. However, this may only be possible if there is a good degree of data management and control. The second model is to centralise the data function, bringing all the 'data people' and report writers into a central team.

The problem with having a large data team all working on the 'information problem' means that the rest of the organisation knows that there is a large team all working on the 'information problem', so why do they need to do anything about it? You start to take on the ownership of the problem, so it looks like it all comes down to you, rather than eliciting a data revolution in which everyone plays a part. Perhaps, rather than 50 people flogging themselves to death to turn the organisation's equivalent of a tanker around, wouldn't it be easier for potentially thousands to all lend a hand? How much more powerful a change do you need than your data stewards infecting all your information champions with enthusiasm, which in turn infects the rest of their department? We know that sounds a bit disease-like, but we like to think of it more like spreading a flame of good data management and governance rather than the slow, rotting decline into the pit of disinterest.

Other roles

There are several other key roles in the CDO team, whichever structure is adopted. Some of these roles may be brought in by the FCDO or may come as the value-add with the SCDO.

We've mentioned data engineers, people to manipulate data, build and manage the ETL; these engineers may also be/include data modellers. It is quite likely that, upon arrival in post, the FCDO will find many people across the organisation 'engineering data' in spreadsheets and Microsoft Access databases. They do this because the data they are given doesn't fit the report that they are trying to build. The data comes as separate data sets, unjoined, with different references, and they are using inappropriate tools, for lack of anything better. If data is the 'new oil', then it should be handled with care, its value recognised, by trained experts with the correct tools.

Data miners, data scientists, call them what you like, will need to be brought in to meet the aspirations of the CEO or board to embrace predictive analytics, machine learning, AI or big data. These are buzz-words that will be driving some behaviour high up in the business. And quite rightly so: organisations are sitting on endless opportunities in their business, locked up in the data, and appropriately skilled and trained people will be needed to unlock this value. It may be hard to recruit the people with this skill set, so the CDO may have to be creative and plan early to up-skill or retrain current colleagues, or lean into organisations or universities who can and will support these activities.

In the past year we have been aware of the importance of having a communications function dedicated within the CDO team. So much of the FCDO's success is dependent on top-class communications, telling the story, winning the hearts and minds, as well as sharing the successes. These all will be a key part of creating a data culture, so a dedicated resource in communications to create the communications strategy as a core part of the overall data strategy is essential.

Inevitably the CDO team will embrace reporting and analytics. This covers the whole spectrum from management information to business intelligence (leaving the predictive analytics, machine learning and AI to the data scientists). These individuals may be out in the business, but their source of data, methodology, governance and even tooling should be derived from the core CDO team. You may feed them or look after them; either way, you will be making sure they have what they need to do their job.

We are seeing that data scientists are of increasing value to the CDO team. This is because they bring a huge range of skills. A data scientist is skilled at finding data, moving data, transforming data, storing data, processing data and then, finally, using data in data visualisation, machine learning, analytics or supplying to another consumer. Additionally, a good data scientist understands the importance of knowing and governing the data, they are very aware of 'garbage in, garbage out' and they need to be able to explain to third parties what the data is and where it came from. On top of this, data scientists are very good at asking questions and being creative. Where they may fall down is on business subject-matter expertise. However, with that broad range of skills a data scientist can perform many roles across the team, from data engineering, to data governance, to machine learning. A team of data scientists may be able to evolve and change their own shape as a team as the data maturity of the business grows and the demands on the data team change. Data scientists may be a shrewd investment for the present and the future of the CDO's data team.

A growing understanding of the breadth of the data scientist's true skills is good for the data science community's longer-term career prospects. This breadth of skills and experience makes them obvious choices to be future CDOs.

The CDO will need creative people: people who can 'ask the question' that the rest of us don't even realise we need to ask; people who can see the patterns and the anomalies in the data; the people with the new ideas. Perhaps these are the people who can see around the corners.

Mark Cuban, the American businessman, investor, author, television personality and philanthropist, suggested that the future demand will be for those who can make sense of the data that automation is spitting out. No, not data scientists. Cuban believes that employers will soon be on the hunt for candidates who excel at creative and critical thinking:

> 'I personally think there's going to be a greater demand in ten years for liberal arts majors than for programming majors and maybe even engineering,' Cuban said. He cited degrees such as English, philosophy, and foreign languages as being the most valuable. 'Maybe not now,' Cuban acquiesced. 'They're gonna starve for awhile. Their day, though, is likely coming.'
>
> (Mark Cuban, in an interview with *Bloomberg TV*)

We think that it may be nearer than many realise. One of the best people we have worked with in 'data' over the past five years had a first-class degree in Philosophy. The people you need around you are those that have a wonderful, relentless curiosity about them and whose main motivation is finding the next wicked problem to solve.

What a success if you can find the creative data scientist! Perhaps this is the unicorn?

Unicorns

Finally, if you can get your hands on a unicorn, then be sure to grab hold of it. At this point you could go and find yourself a mythical beast that looks like a horse with a horn on its head, or you could realise that we are talking about that (almost) equally hard-to-find creature that will do some amazing things with your data while you protect them from anyone wanting to enforce procedure in what they do.

The hard part is that we don't believe you can 'catch your unicorn' – we believe you grow them. Finding a unicorn is as rare as the stars aligning and you winning the lottery, and then, even if you get them, how do you know they can work their magic in your business? Would a more sensible proposition not be to create a high-performing team culture and give everyone the potential to become a unicorn?

The high-performing team

There are some basic rules about what you can do to create this type of team and encourage people to stretch and grow into the best versions of themselves:

- Communicate the vision and direction of the team: we cannot stress this enough; the team need to be on the same page, all pulling in the same direction; you cannot over-communicate, keep people focused on that data nirvana you are moving them towards. It is so easy for people to get distracted or take a wrong turn, but it is your role to stay on message and keep them on track. You might have unicorns that look like they are doing something completely different, but you need to trust them, because if you have created a clear enough vision they are just looking for different (better) paths to get there, or are challenging your vision because they have something to add to it. People will want to join a team with energy, passion, a mission and a vision . . . and a great leader.

- Trust: the old phrase about trust is so true – it takes ages to build and seconds to wipe out – so obviously this doesn't come overnight, but you need to set the standard when it comes to trust. Being trustworthy is a really good start – and displaying trust in your team. It is truly amazing what people can achieve when they are sure their manager 'has their back'.
- Stretch your team: people love the idea that they can do something extraordinary. Setting goals that are achievable helps people to recognise their own strength and improves their pride in themselves and their team, making them want to do even more.
- Pull, don't push.
- Resolve conflicts, increase co-operation: every team goes through the 'forming, storming, norming, performing' process in some way, shape or form. All of these phases have value and are necessary in order for the team to grow, face up to challenges, tackle problems and find solutions. At the same time we often expect mature people to sort out differences on their own, but we need to create a way of resolving differences quickly and to promote co-operation within the team.

One other consideration you need to think of when you are putting your team together is to make sure people have the opportunity to grow and stretch themselves within the team and beyond. Some roles lend themselves to following on from each other – the data analyst to data steward is one simple example – but understanding what the possibilities are, coupled with information about the people, will help you to help them in the best way. As roles become more and more professionalised there are pathways to help you with this progression, such as the work CILIP (Chartered Institute of Library and Information Professionals) has completed around career progression and professional development. Up-skilling internally is hugely important. If you accept that we are going to need armies of data scientists, this will be a demand that is hard to beat, so growing your own has to be a good idea. We have recently seen the success of in-house programmes to train people from the line of business, including HR, Marketing, Audit, Compliance and Finance in the basics of data science. Some go on to train further for a career in data science, once bitten by the bug; others return to their line of business with a new awareness of data and its power and are capable of framing the data questions in their everyday jobs, bringing huge value to their domains.

Bring these skills in-house if you possibly can. Grow the capability within your own team, who know and understand your data and your business.

Your team is the most important asset you will have; they will have a massive impact on how successful you will be and they are potentially the CDOs of the future.

11
The next 300 days

Introduction

This chapter looks at the imperatives for the CDO after the first 100 days in post. It stresses the importance of getting back to the strategic. This chapter is very much aimed at the CDO; however, it can also be a useful read for the early members of the CDO team to help understand what is going to happen next.

You've now got through the first 100 days, settled into a new business, met your new colleagues, got a first impression of the data environment and the state of the nation and carried out your own assessment of the maturity of the data environment. You're probably bursting with ideas and plans. In our experience you will have spoken to more people than you can remember and been in a lifetime of meetings and will have many notebooks full of writing. That is the only way to throw your arms around what is going on and to make a true assessment of the data estate and processes. You will also have spent 100 days listening carefully so as to understand the direction and aspirations of the business.

While things will obviously look different depending on what generation of CDO you are, the steps are the same. An SCDO might be able to skip through some of them faster, but if you miss the steps altogether, how confident can you be that you are standing on firm foundations? The FCDO Replayed may need to take longer over some of the earlier steps, such as ... assessing data maturity or building a data governance framework to meet the challenges of either the earlier failure of a CDO or a reset of the organisation's data journey.

The next three steps

This is the moment to do three things, and they are sequential.

First: draw a breath and take a moment to pull all the thoughts and those meetings together, review the notes you have taken and make an assessment of the state of the data maturity and what needs to be done. The following are the points to measure against:

1   **Reporting and analytics**. Is this efficient, how many reports are produced and who for? It is a good idea if possible to calculate the FTE hours expended on reporting, the number of reports and cost per report. Assess the reporting: is it management information or business intelligence, is any analytics or data science going on?

2   **Information flows**. How is information used throughout the organisation? It is time to start understanding the physical, logical and conceptual data models of the business. A good measure of the data maturity is the existing state and clarity of these models.

3   **Data governance**. What structures or frameworks are in place, is there an information asset register and are there clearly defined and properly functional data owners? What is the data maturity? How is accountability viewed?

4   **Data management**. Lineage, models and maturity of metadata; is the data mastered and governed?

5   **Data organisational design.** Is reporting and data management centralised, is it federated and democratised across the business or is it in separate silos? What capability and skills exist within the business for data management, reporting and analytics?

6   **Data technology.** What is there, how is it used, is it fit for purpose? Are there proper ETL tools and data stores? Is there a functioning data layer? Does IT or the business understand the concept of a data layer?

This should give you a good starting point to make your top-level assessment of the state of the nation. We have found that even after the 300 days it is worth revisiting this checklist again. Take some time out and challenge yourself with these points. It is easy to get drawn into the weeds and then into the deep water, and to lose sight of that strategic big picture. Take the time to look up and reflect, it will be invaluable.

Second: create a story around this, have the detail and examples, and play the current situation back to your stakeholders. However dire you may think the current situation is, the business has been operating and working with data and there should be some positives which you can play back as well, so that it isn't all about disaster. This is a good time to play back the data maturity assessment. Make sure you don't run around yelling that 'the sky is falling'. But do let people know where the real problems lie. We would guess that your C-Suite colleagues are probably already aware of the symptoms but are not really aware of, or don't understand, the underlying causes of the symptoms. At the same time, give them your view of the future, how to deal with the burning issues, the tactical plan (immediate data strategy or IDS) and the more strategic view (target data strategy, TDS). Perhaps this is the time to discuss the hype cycle, or the Carruthers & Jackson CDO Journey with your senior colleagues. This is the moment when you should be stepping out onto the Table of Enlightenment. It is essential that you take your colleagues along the 'Table' journey so that the real story is managed with a controlled drop off the Cliff of Reality.

Third: draw back from the business slightly, it is time to think and plan. The start of the 300 days is the time to bring your data team around you, either by recruitment or by internal moves. It is time to identify your SWAT team and your transformation team, and to decide on the shape of your final data organisational design. You will need support around you to get through the next 300 days.

Tasks to be achieved

There are two high-level tasks that should be achieved in the next 300 days.

1 Deliver the IDS, the tactical fixes; you will have one eye on the hype cycle, or on securing your transition to the stage of Accelerating Delivery and Value. What these tactical fixes are will largely depend on your context and the outcomes of your 100-day assessment.
2 Write the TDS and have it in the starting blocks, ready to commence the transformation and ready to deliver.

Achieving these two together can be tough, hence the need to gather your data team around you.

Delivering the IDS

For the tactical area, build on the work you did in your first 100 days. Find the real pain points; you'll probably find a cluster with the same root cause that can be addressed with one tactical solution. Be honest with the business and inform them that this is tactical; inform them of any limitations and dependencies. Tell the business what you are not going to do and why; tell them when it will get done, if it is part of the data strategy; and, as much as you can, make your tactical fixes a building block in your long-term plans. If you can make those tactical moves fit with a strategic future, minimise the regret spend and don't build up too much data debt to be unpicked later on.

This is where your skills as the CDO appear: the ability to communicate, the subject expertise to weigh up the problem and think creatively about a solution, or to know whom to consult and then be able to assess the advice. But, as well, be able to weigh up the impact for the business of fixing or not fixing a problem. There may be 'hidden' value in demonstrating the art of the possible to the business. It is very possible that you will have a backlog that is overwhelming; there may be many burning platforms or pressures or a lot of low-hanging fruit, so you will need to create a transparent method for prioritisation that is driven by the business. After all, your role is to deliver business value and great business outcome.

Delivering the IDS will get lots of plates spinning and lots of people involved; you will be like the ringmaster in a multi-ring circus. Oh, and bear in mind that the business must keep going, and watch out for the naysayers!

This will inevitably bring you into contact with Procurement. The level of governance will depend on your sector and business, but, whatever your context, try to establish a good relationship with a procurement business partner; set their expectations of your plans and the pace at which you wish to deliver. Many data tools are SaaS (software as a service) and cloud based; Procurement may be another part of the business that you are educating about new and different licence models and subscriptions.

Inevitably the tactical work will lean heavily towards adopting an agile approach, but unless the business is well practised in agile methodology you may need to keep a foot in both camps, both agile and waterfall - developing some high-level requirements, which might be best articulated as use cases, and establishing some project milestones and deliverables. Our advice through the IDS delivery is: promise less and deliver more. You will want to get the data project off to a good start, and the best way is to start small and build on it. We realise it is radical to go against the over-promise and under-deliver model that most businesses seem to live by, but your life will be a lot easier if you try the under-promise and over-deliver way of working.

Working on the TDS

Think about how you are going to resource the IDS and the work on the TDS. You might need two teams with a level of temporary support. Remember that you can draw on resources from the business: you don't have to just rely on direct reports to you - get creative about how you get things done!

The TDS will need to work closely with the business on its needs and requirements. What is the strategic vision for the company, what principles underpin this and how can it be delivered? Work with IT to look at new technology; work with Procurement and HR and the change function; focus on creating that sustainable change in the business.

Create check points through the 300 days on delivery of the TDS. It's much easier to realise that you are wandering off track if you have little milestones that make you stop and think. It's also much easier to course-correct during the work rather than looking back once it is completed and wondering how you ended up in the wrong place.

One of the biggest traps that you will be tempted into in the first year is to get down and dirty with the detail. There will be lots of things to work with, and your job is to understand the coverage, not the detail. Try to keep that at arm's length; trust your team and keep your focus on making their path easier for them. Therefore it's essential to be able to recruit good people with the right skills and experience and then to trust and empower them to deliver.

12
The different generations of Chief Data Officers

Introduction

This chapter examines the idea that there are two types of CDO; the first-generation CDO (FCDO) and the second-generation CDO (SCDO). We go on to discuss their roles and deliverables.

An evolving role

The CDO is an evolving role and, as such, there are different 'flavours' of CDO, who are still all about the data but maybe come at the problem from different directions. We find there are few things in life where 'one size fits all', so why should we assume that one CDO will solve all our problems? The simple answer is that they won't, and while there are many different varieties (being the wonderful, multifaceted humans we are), currently they can be loosely categorised into two groups: first-and second-generation CDOs. Before we jump into the current CDOs, we look at where the role came from.

Every C-Suite role had come from somewhere, believe it or not the CFO wasn't a core component of the strategic team. The very first CDO was in 2002 for Capital One, with a slightly eclectic responsibility for IT, Supply Chain and Market Analyses – nothing about getting value from the data. The banking industry picked up on CDOs faster than any other industry, focusing them on the governance side of the role, but by then the uptake of CDOs had begun. Data from Forbes shows that by 2012 only 12% of Fortune 1000 companies had a CDO, but by 2018 this had grown to just under 70%, and the number continues to rise. Countries are now getting the idea. France was the first European country to have a CDO, in 2014, closely followed by the UK in 2015. In 2019 every state in the US was tasked with having a CDO of their very own, so it's fair to say that the role is more established. However, this hasn't stopped the evolution of the role and, as more people from varied backgrounds bring their experience to bear, the role will continue to evolve. As we discussed in Chapter 2, this evolution has even resulted in the FCDO Replayed. Perhaps this is even a re-evolution.

First-generation versus second-generation CDOs

In the same way that Steve Jobs and his team developed the very first Apple computer, viewing it as a set of components, the FCDO has to adopt a similar view within an organisation, to see it as a large, complex beast that does what it needs to (hopefully), but not necessarily with finesse, with lots of disparate bits of data and information existing without any thought of connectivity. Not so much a lovely governed data lake, more of a children's playing field on a rainy Saturday afternoon, filled with sodden holes trying desperately to join up to form little streams.

The SCDO, on the other hand, has these foundations to build upon, but the company has been patient (possibly) while they were being built and ready to get some value from the work it has undertaken, and so the SCDO has to drive the value from the data to help the organisation thrive.

The two generations of CDO are different, but obviously have a great deal in common. If we break this down simply, imagine a pendulum that swings between complete risk aversion at one end of the scale and total value-add at the other (see Figure 12.1). It would be rare that you would sit completely at one end of the scale or the other. Every place on the scale has merit and any one might be the best fit for your organisation. What you need to decide is where on this scale you fit. If you lean towards the risk aversion end, you are probably first generation, and if you lean towards the value-add side you are second generation. You should never forget about both ends of the scale, but you will at least know where your focus has to be.

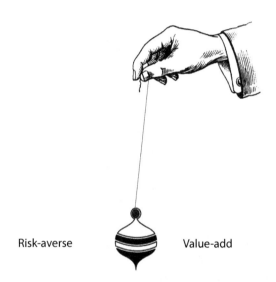

Risk-averse   Value-add

Figure 12.1 *The risk-averse/value-add pendulum*

First-generation CDOs

A true FCDO will be the first individual in that organisation with the title of CDO and with the responsibility for data across the enterprise and, with it, a burden of expectations. This role will not have existed previously in the organisation. If this is the case, then the true FCDO will not have a ready-structured team and their colleagues will not be quite sure what to expect. However, there is a second type of FCDO: those CDOs who take over a data strategy that is in the process of being set up. They may follow on from another FCDO who was the first incumbent but who left before the data strategy hit BAU. This type of FDCO probably will inherit an embryonic data team and will find lots of data transformations in place. Whether or not the data team or the transformations are well developed and progressed is irrelevant; these CDOs are also really FCDOs (perhaps replayed). They have to maintain the quick wins, deliver the strategy and keep the communications and relationship building going. In some ways their task is harder than their predecessor's because they are delivering someone else's strategy, and a big change of direction could unnerve an organisation that may be still understanding the vision of the previous CDO. Whether they are a true FCDO or an FCDO Replayed, they will have an organisation that is evolving around them as they start to open up the 'data conversation' and the data literacy starts to improve (if they are being successful at their job). All of a sudden the organisational light-bulb moment may happen and the FCDO may be asked 'why are we moving so slowly?' The Trough of Disillusion may suddenly appear, because the organisation has evolved and expectations have risen.

The role of the FCDO is daunting but satisfying, full of quick wins, as siloed pockets of data are pulled together (often kicking and screaming at first) to form coherent pieces of information. The first generation is all about 'getting the basics right', demonstrating what can happen when you start to treat your data as an asset and understand its potential.

One of the hardest things to overcome as an FCDO is that all of a sudden the organisation has invested in a key asset (you) and they want something to happen. They want this something to happen NOW, preferably, but next week would be okay at a push. It doesn't matter how long the organisation has been set up – it will have developed its own complex way of working and you will need to understand what makes it tick before you do something irreversible. So, setting expectations is a very wise first step. That said, you can't sit around for the next two years and expect the organisation to wait while you ponder your navel. So, as with any new role, the FCDO needs to take a breath, to get the lie of the land, understand the big picture and get on with it!

You actually need to focus on four key areas:

- governance
- information architecture

- engagement
- building capability

and the quick wins . . . what are the blinding flashes of the obvious that other people just haven't had the time for, have left to someone else or have been consigned to the 'too-hard box'.

There's a lot more detail about these key areas in Chapter 5, but don't assume that you need to worry about them only in the first 100 days – they have a life beyond that time period too. Governance, information architecture, capability and engagement are for life, not just for the first 100 days. They will help you when you are thinking about demonstrating the value that you and your team bring to the company. They give you the background to deliver that tangible value to make organisations believe they're on the right path.

The FCDO will also be thinking about 'data technology'. This may play a role in the quick wins – see Chapter 7 on avoiding the hype cycle. Data technology will certainly play a leading role in the information strategy which is to follow and will be part of the FCDO's longer-term delivery. Just remember not to get sucked into thinking the technology will solve all your problems for you – that's partially how businesses have got into this mess in the first place. Technology is just a tool to help you, not a panacea for all the ills of the data world.

Although the FCDO will probably sit on the risk-averse end of the pendulum swing, there will be occasions when risk must and will be embraced, but a good FCDO will manage this risk so that it isn't destabilising to the wider business. One method of venturing confidently into what could be risky territory is to deliver minimal viable products. So, the FCDO may engage in what may seem risky and very innovative and entrepreneurial initiatives, but the risk is managed. This means that, unlike with a PoC, you will be reducing your regret spend, as you are creating something that can be industrialised but still provides value at this early stage of its life cycle.

The FCDO will have particular necessary strengths if they want to specialise as an FCDO. They will need to be optimistic, full of energy, able to think around problems and solve them, and able to face the same issues and problems as they move from position to position. This is an exacting role and will take its toll, so we would expect to see some FCDOs morph into SCDOs, staying in the same position to reap the benefits of their hard work and slog. An FCDO who is good at this may become a specialist FCDO Replayed.

> I also think that organisation structure is key to both CDO generations. The first one sorts out how the organisation is serviced by data i.e. some sort of BI/Analytics competency centre. This is mainly down to the quick wins that the first gen has to achieve and I think the pressures from the board etc. are unreasonable. The first generation have to do a lot with a little budget – education is the key here. Data Governance is a big deal for many orgs as they find it difficult to embed the change that is required to place the controls around data. Often, many CDOs fail at this and this isn't down to them – more company culture and messaging not trickling down from the top. For the second generation CDO, I think they are able to step back, look at the organisation, create a more lasting and fulfilling data strategy (on their terms), and work with the business for more profound change. This often leads to your 'vision' point – they can be more artistic and experimentation is appreciated more so by the business. They also know that investing in data quality/engineering is where you can achieve more of the 'art of the possible' and change starts to happen quicker as people see the benefits. The culture becomes more proactive in its uses of data and less siloed. I still think there is a massive alignment that needs to happen with CDOs and their C-Suite colleagues – and many need to be on equal par to succeed.
>
> (Samir Sharma, Data Strategy and Analytics Expert)

Second-generation CDOs

The role of the second-generation CDO is no less daunting than that of the FCDO, but from a different perspective. Yes, you have to kick the tyres and make sure the car runs, but you are now faced with making the vehicle perform like an F1 machine. Your organisation has already been sold the vision of what it can be with great data governance, and all the value that can be derived from the data – now you have to deliver it!

One of the hardest things to overcome as an SCDO is that all of a sudden the organisation has invested in a key asset (you) and they want something to happen. Now, preferably, but next week would be okay at a push. Sounds familiar?

If you are lucky and a rock star of an FCDO has sorted out the basics for you, excellent! You could rely on everything you are told and start doing your job, *or* you could take just a few moments to check that your foundations are as solid, well built and sized right as you had hoped. Again, the same advice holds – you need to understand what makes something tick before you do something irreversible. For you, it just means that it's a check and maybe a few tweaks, rather than a wholescale delivery programme.

We have proposed that an SCDO turns the 'possible' into an art form, 'understanding the nuances of the family and making the house a home filled with wonder and intelligence'.

The FCDO who landed in the brownfield site hopefully will have cleared the site and built good foundations. In data terms this will mean that an effective data governance framework is in place and operational, and that the technology is in place to manage and master the data. The SCDO has a responsibility to maintain the foundations and keep abreast of technology innovations; however, the SCDO should also be seeking to deliver real value into the business.

The predecessor will probably have delivered the single-customer view, mastered the asset management and created a process for maintaining the quality of the data. With these essentials in place the SCDO can bring additional value in a number of ways:

- **Advanced analytics and data science**. The FCDO will have created an environment (collecting, storage and management) where data can be extracted and used or advanced analytics applied to provide customer or operational insight for obvious value to the business through increased revenue, greater efficiency, reduced costs or increased market share.
- **Data narrative**. The SCDO will be able to provide narrative around the data. They will be able to make the data tell a story.
- **Data visualisation**. The FCDO will have established quality, governed data that can be used in data visualisations to communicate messages about business progress or provide management information.
- **Publishing data**. The SCDO will be able to be transparent with data and publish it, either back to the client, into the business, to a regulator or into the public domain, because he or she has a

complete understanding of the provenance and quality of the data.

- **Data refining**. The SCDO will be able to gain greater insight and value from the data, whether that is through monetisation or through really driving an effective, data-driven business transformation.

If you find that you are devoting much of your time to these sorts of initiatives then you are probably an SCDO. In effect, though, you may be a hybrid FCDO and SCDO, or transitioning your organisation from FCDO to SCDO. The SCDO will be able to take more risks, be agile, fail quickly and then achieve success fast, because of the solid work done by the FCDO.

The SCDO may need to change or augment the shape and volume of the data team. For example, this may be the time to start building a strong data science capability. Engagement is still key at this point, in fact there is no time when it's not fundamental, there will just be a shift in engagement, away from driving the change and towards letting the organisation get the best from the new capabilities it has.

The SCDO may have the opportunity to be truly innovative, and have the space to look over the horizon and beyond, starting to embrace more challenging ideas and data-driven operating models. The SCDO may even establish a research and development team separate from the main operational team to push these boundaries, really driving the pace of change from a strategic point of view.

When an organisation recruits an SCDO it needs to be very aware of the strengths and skills required. It may be that the SCDO leans more to the reporting, analytics and data science end of the skill set, with a dose of data modelling and data governance, but has a weaker suit in the data management technologies.

Third-generation CDOs

We've talked about the FCDOs and SCDOs, so what next? We have all heard that some think that the CDO role is just a gimmick that companies are being sold, that it won't actually help them in any way or that once they have all the data organised there will no longer be any need for a CDO and the position will fade away, leaving us with the more traditional roles making up the C-Suite. To address the first point, since the first edition of this book came out the number of CDOs around the world has continued to grow – just look at the Forbes statistics at the beginning of this chapter – and there is no sign that this is slowing down. As we have come to recognise that data is an asset, so it is also becoming recognised that you need a strategic leader who has the responsibility to look after and drive value from that asset across the whole organisation, in the same way that your CFO does for your finances.

Regarding the idea that data can be fixed and then you won't need a CDO any more, it's not really that simple. While this is a nice, neat ending – it's always great to have something come full circle: identify a need, solve the problem and everyone goes home – we don't believe that it is as simple as that. It feels at times as if data is a living, breathing organism which constantly morphs and seems to follow the laws of evolution. To expand the analogy, it is the business which is the organism and the data that is the lifeblood that runs within it, making sure everything works the way it is supposed to. Nothing, literally nothing, works in a company without the input of data in some shape or form. Any business which receives data from another organisation, or shares data with another organisation, will constantly be faced with 'data challenges' that need addressing, from their systems getting a refresh or replacement, to their data being sourced from a new supplier or partner. It may be that the business operation changes to meet a market reform or regulatory change. Just think of GDPR, and you will understand how an outside factor can be disrupting to the internal data environment. So, there will always be a role for someone to be in charge of an organisation's data.

If the FCDO takes this data and makes it trustworthy and relevant, and the SCDO derives the value from it, what would a third-generation CDO or beyond have to do? Do we just stick at a second generation, or assume that companies can cope on their own now?

We have talked about the ever-increasing problem that is data; estimates are that 85% of the data we collect is irrelevant, or should be deleted and could be wasting companies the equivalent of over US$3.1 trillion every year (IBM estimate, Harvard Business Review, September 2016). So, even when you have got something that big under control, do you expect it to stay in the nice little box that each organisation put it in? Honestly, we can't see it. Data wouldn't have become such a problem in the first place if businesses were capable of dealing with it on its own (and we are taking the liberty here of assuming they couldn't, though some smaller organisations that manage their own data effectively won't need a CDO - that part comes down to business strategy). The CDO position arose from a genuine, enterprise-level business need, so we think that we will see larger, complex businesses needing a CDO in some shape or form going forward.

It is that 'shape or form' which we believe is up for debate. It would be easy at this point to say something glib like 'we never know what the future holds', and, while there is always truth in that statement, we are supposed to be the pioneers in this area, so for us to just hold up our hands and say we haven't got a clue feels cowardly. Bear with us while we skip around a little bit, but there are lots of predictions about how many CDOs will be seen as failures (approximately 50%, depending on who you ask), and that ties in with the point we are talking about. There will be lots of reasons for this failure: round pegs in square holes, culture clashes, competing demands - the list can go on. One reason for failure is the same reason why many big programmes fail: companies don't have a clear idea of what they want the CDO to do. They may have a really clear idea of what they don't want to happen any more - data failures, wasting money, safety-critical decisions not being made - but few have a clear idea of what the utopian data future will bring or what it looks like. Since the business doesn't know what it wants, the CDO becomes a bit of a hot potato: where do they put this new person? Under the CIO, direct to the CEO, or any other myriad places?

By the time of the third-generation CDO (TCDO) this will be more normalised across organisations. The successful FCDOs and SCDOs will lead the way, and, as companies learn what works and what doesn't, the role will become less pioneering and more established. We are already seeing TCDOs taking their place at the helm of multinational companies, as well as the first set of these CDOs moving into Chief Operating Officer (COO) or CEO roles because it has become one of the few strategic-level roles which allows you the ability to scan the breadth of an organisation, rather than focus on the silos.

We shied away from calling the earliest CDOs among us 'cowboys', but we did talk about pioneers in what can feel like either a wasteland or an overcrowded cattle drive. We are not saying they aren't professional, but by the third generation the role is professionalised. Data and information management is a recognised discipline, in the way that project management or architecture are; we are starting to see data with its own certifications adding to the professionalism of the sector. Having a recognised professional accreditation for an information professional, for instance, lets you know exactly what you are getting for your money. A 'chartership' gives you not only the standard but the ethical quality that the person has signed up to. This will apply to all the new roles that the CDO brings with them. How much easier it will be when you not only have a rough idea of what kind of shape your team will need to take, but also have recognised roles about which you can have sensible conversations with your HR team or recruiters when you need to add to your collective hoard. Tailoring your job descriptions will always take time, but it is nice to have something to start tailoring with. Blank pages are slightly terrifying, and typically end up with a cut-and-paste job that includes elements that can be off-putting to the pool you are fishing from.

The skill set of the TCDO will be understood and professionalised and the skill set will be a capability that can be rigorously assessed. If the other roles in the data revolution are formalised then the CDO must also embrace the regularisation of what we do. Currently one of the main questions we get asked is 'What does a CDO do?' Can you imagine anyone asking a Chief Information Officer what they do? (Actually, considering the conversation we had about the CIO role in the C-Suite, let's pick a different C-Suite role!) Our ambition is to make the CDO role as recognisable as roles such as the Chief Financial Officer – while you get different flavours you know the rough shape of what the role is aimed at. As that role changes and develops, so too must the CDOs. Now if you keep hold of that pioneering, agile and flexible spirit then you will cope fine with the transition. There is a whole load of evolution for the role and you will have to keep morphing the shape of what you do without modifying the core – never forget you are there to advocate for the data and the value you can get from it. While we are still being asked these questions, they are coming from a different level of understanding now, whereas the majority before was 'what does a CDO do?' now the focus tends towards the 'How can I get the best from a CDO?' Another way to think about the evolution into the FCDO is that the job title and description may change. If the previous two generations have been successful in their jobs; if data is governed and effective data ownership is in place, if data is accessible, if the right data tools are deployed, if capability has been built then the TCDO may be truly value adders and may be Chief Analytics Officers or Chief Data Scientists.

A closing thought: the FCDOs and SCDOs that are part of the successful 50% will become the data heroes. Some of these will have the potential to move on into other C-Suite roles such as COO and CEO because they blend the data skills and business skills, are capable of strategic thinking, driving and delivering transformation and can win the hearts and minds of organisations. We want to expand that 50% so that many more CDOs are viewed as successful, hence why we wrote this book. When we treat our data correctly, everyone wins.

13
What type of Chief Data Officer are you?

Introduction

This chapter poses a number of questions: are you an FCDO or an SCDO? CDOs come from a wide spectrum of skills and experience: where are you on that spectrum? What are your strengths and weaknesses? We discuss the importance of addressing these questions. The questions may be too simple, or perhaps the answers more complex than it might seem. There are several features that will determine what type of CDO you are.

What sort of CDO?

Looking at one aspect, which we have discussed already, are you an FCDO, SCDO or TCDO? Each of these is very different, regardless of their background, expertise or sector. The difference is very much around what type of person you are. In very simple terms, as an FCDO you will probably arrive in post with no existing team, reports or support. It may well be that you don't even have a desk because your role hasn't existed before. The FCDO isn't on the auto-invite for the many meetings and boards that they need to be on, so the role is often a lonely one for a while: the person in that role has to be resilient, able to think and motivate themselves alone, and to be very outgoing, to win the hearts and minds within the organisation. You would really struggle with this role as a shrinking violet. The SCDO and TCDO can perhaps be more low key, even though they will want to make their own mark; they will at least have a warm desk and a team to welcome them, and perhaps a budget. The organisation should already understand their value and the types of return on investment that they can bring.

CDOs come from many backgrounds and have a variety of skills. It is worth spending some time to consider what sort of CDO you are. What sort of CDO will you be, or wish to be? Or, if you are running a business, what sort of CDO do you want, or what sort do you wish to recruit? It is especially important to understand this, both for the recruiter and for the recruit; this will be make or break, both at interview and in post. It is very possible to get the 'wrong' CDO, and it is wise for any organisation looking for a CDO to get specialist help from a recruiter who has expertise in this field and is well connected, so that they understand the business's needs and what is available in the market that is relevant to them.

Patterns of CDOs' backgrounds

Let's take a look at some of the common differences among CDOs.

When we wrote the first edition of this book there were four clear backgrounds that a CDO tended to come from, and you could normally fit CDOs into these categories:

- Are you a technology-led CDO? Does your strength lie in expertise in the technology of data? If so, be sure to gather around you the strengths of data governance and reporting and analytics. The technology-led CDO is a good play. Many projects can be rescued or driven to success by the appropriate use of data technology. The experience you have regarding project, programme and portfolio management, along with stakeholder and change management, will serve you well.

- Are you a data-/information-led CDO? This is an individual who majors on data models, data architecture and data lineage. This might be the hardest background to project into the role of CDO, but we would be surprised if an individual with these skills didn't at least have a strong second string in either technology or governance.
- Do your strengths emanate from good general management and leadership skills? If this is the case, as a CDO you will need to be surrounded by very trusted data subject experts. It may be that individuals like this are better suited to being CEO or COO and then bring on board a CDO! The same could be said of an individual with excellent business skills.
- In some situations there will be CDOs who are the entrepreneur/start-up/innovator/disruptor CDO. These are the ones who are able to drive change through pure, agile methodology, who are capable of getting the business to try lots and fail fast; the ones who can create a blame-free culture of innovation. Other CDOs of this type will have a background focused on programme management and delivery. They will have been involved in transformation programmes. The very process of becoming a data-driven business will involve transformation and excellent programme management and stakeholder engagement.
- Some CDOs will come from an analytics background and have strengths around finding insights in data.
- Others may come from a background in risk.

Each one of these categories had strengths and weaknesses to bring to the role at a time when many applicants were from a technology background. They were former CTOs or similar who wanted to move into 'data' for one reason or another. They were technically pretty competent, though in a few cases their 'data technology' awareness may not have been their strength. The bulk of other applicants tended to be from a regulatory background, especially financial services. So they were strong on data governance and GDPR, but not so strong on technology. Both of those groups could be weak on data strategy, reporting and analytics and data science.

Our original diagram (Figure 13.1) also included the idea of the unicorn, that could do anything equally as well. We have yet to see one of those in the flesh! The idea of being able to do it all recedes even further when you take into account the wider variety now seen in the applicants for the role. It is important to note, however, that as a CDO it isn't enough to just be a data leader, you have to be a business leader as well. Remember, the role is about looking at how you get the best from your data assets strategically across the whole business. Being a guru in Python doesn't cut it; you have to be able to apply context to your skills in order to really make a difference.

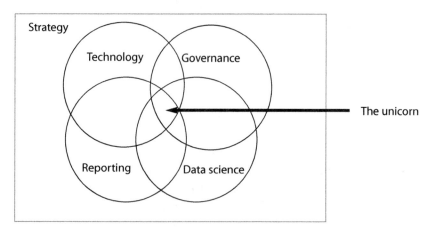

Figure 13.1 *Attributes of a unicorn Chief Data Officer*

There have definitely been changes and we are seeing a much broader appeal of the CDO role to applicants that you might not expect. The category that has seen a great increase is from an operational background, and while they don't have a strong data background, they do understand data within the organisation. They obviously have an advantage when it comes to understanding the business and have probably got a wealth of things that they are looking to change and improve - they might just need a little help with the data side.

We've even seen cases of MBA students coming straight in as a CDO to be a change agent without having a data background. However, the only time that has been successful is when the MBA student already worked for the company, and so have a great grounding in what needed to be achieved. This does open up another consideration for you and companies to think about. Are you a change agent? If so, is your focus on being a rock star CDO who can move from company to company creating the change and then moving on when a BAU state is achieved; or do you intimately understand the business and are you assuming the CDO mantle for a period of time because that is what will drive your company forward? Again, each has its place, but if you are the former, then you need to make sure you have people from the business propping you up, and if you are internal, then please make sure you bring in a right-hand person who knows data. Offset your areas of challenge and play to your strengths. There is lots to be said for both, but the main thing is understanding yourself in order to understand the team dynamics you bring in around you.

Interestingly, according to Forbes, currently of the CDOs who have a degree 68% have a business-oriented degree and 40% have a technology-related degree. Now we know that those don't add up to 100%, but you can have more than one degree so we are obviously a bunch of over-achievers.

The landscape looks a little more as shown in Figure 13.2 now, and we are sure this will continue to evolve and finesse, each area bringing an increased richness to the role.

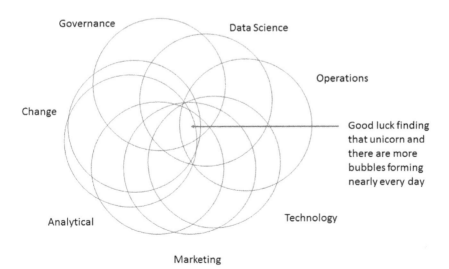

Figure 13.2 *Where does a CDO come from?*

Adapting to the surroundings is very important, as many CDOs move position across sectors. Some move from private sector to public sector, others move across verticals, from fast moving consumer goods to financial or transport and utilities or any combination of these. In fact, this is becoming more and more obvious, and the average length of time for a CDO to stay with one company is around two years. This is partly because the role is in increasing demand, so it is a seller's market, but it is also related to the CDO fulfilling what the organisation needed from a CDO during that time period. We think that CDOs are less defined by their vertical or sectoral orientation and more by their skills or by their 'breed' - FCDO, SCDO or TCDO - as each CDO tends to have strengths they can bring to each situation, as long as they land in the right 'phase' for the organisation.

The importance of understanding your CDO type

In conclusion, it is important that you understand what sort of CDO you are for a number of reasons:

- so that you play to your strengths
- so that you know where your strengths lie and identify your weaker skills. Knowing what sort of CDO you're not is just as important, so that you can either develop those skills or, more practically, recruit the right people to work with you to complement your strengths. Don't assume that you need to be all things to all people; while Mary Poppins was practically perfect in every way, very few of us are and we need teams around us to get the job done well
- to make sure that you apply for/respond to the right job advert that requires your skills. It is crucial that you know what sort of CDO you are, because often the employer, or even the recruiter, may not appreciate the difference between what they are looking for and what you are. Not all CDO roles are the same and not all CDOs are the same. It is like old-fashioned dating without an algorithm to help. It is incumbent on you to know what you are and what you want (and what you are prepared to compromise on).

It is important for the business to understand what sort of CDO they require and why, and to articulate this clearly. If they cannot, then it is important and very worthwhile to engage a recruiter who is able to bottom this out and find the right candidates.

It is therefore important for both the candidate and the business that the recruiters understand that different businesses will require different CDOs, depending on their circumstances, and that there are different types of CDO in the marketplace. Remember the motto: no one size fits all in the data world.

14
How to present yourself as a Chief Data Officer

Introduction

The CDO is still a relatively new role, and while we have moved into having more CDOs who are proven, know their niche and can really lead data within organisations, the role is still evolving. There are major differences in role models and the market for them is still changing. This chapter discusses how you can present yourself as a CDO and how to get help to do so.

Questions to ask yourself

The very first thing you need to ask yourself is why you want to be a CDO. Obviously, we think it is an awesome job and love it, but we also recognise that it's not for everyone. It's always a good idea to check your reasons for wanting to do it, because they are the thing that will carry you forward when the going gets really tough.

Second, who do you think you are? Have you ever asked yourself that question? Whatever answer you give will probably be right, as we tend to become the person we think we are, but the more important question is, who do you want to be? It's critical to know that who you are isn't all that you are capable of being. It really is up to you.

As a small aside here, let's just touch upon values and how they are inextricably linked to our beliefs and behaviours, as it's ultimately committing to a choice of behaviour that we usually need to work on, while maintaining our values and beliefs.

Beliefs are things we hold to be true, values set the standard for what we think is important, and both shape our behaviour (what we actually do). So your belief could be that everyone is essentially good, you value honesty and your behaviour is that you are honest and expect that in others.

Everything we suggest that you try in this chapter has to fit with your values, we aren't suggesting that you become something that is alien to you. Make sure that you understand your non-negotiables - where are the red lines that you aren't prepared to compromise on? It's all an ongoing process, some of which is based upon the past (knowing yourself), but some of which is based upon where/who we want to be - which might be getting access to opportunities that we have never tried before, want to try and might be brilliant at. Don't be afraid of failure; failure is just one aspect of trying.

We'll now take a quick look at Ikigai (Figure 14.1 opposite), a Japanese concept that means 'reason for being', which is sometimes described as having a purpose in life and focuses on the sweet spot where your passion, mission, vocation and profession overlap.

So what does this mean for how you present yourself as a CDO?

Take all this and building on it, what if we looked at it as shown in Figure 14.2.

Are you currently a CDO and, if so, what type? Are you are an FCDO or SCDO, have you been there and done that and know you're a third generation? Go back and read the previous chapter. Where do your talents, strengths, weaknesses, core values, personality and track record lie? It would be a big mistake for you, and your employer, if you are

what you
LOVE
Passion
Mission
what
you are
GOOD
AT
ikigai
what
the World
NEEDS
Profession
Vocation
what
you can be
PAID FOR

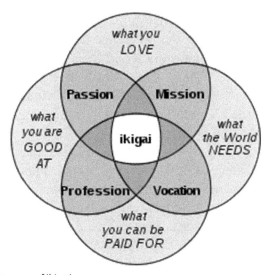

Figure 14.1 *Diagram of Ikigai*

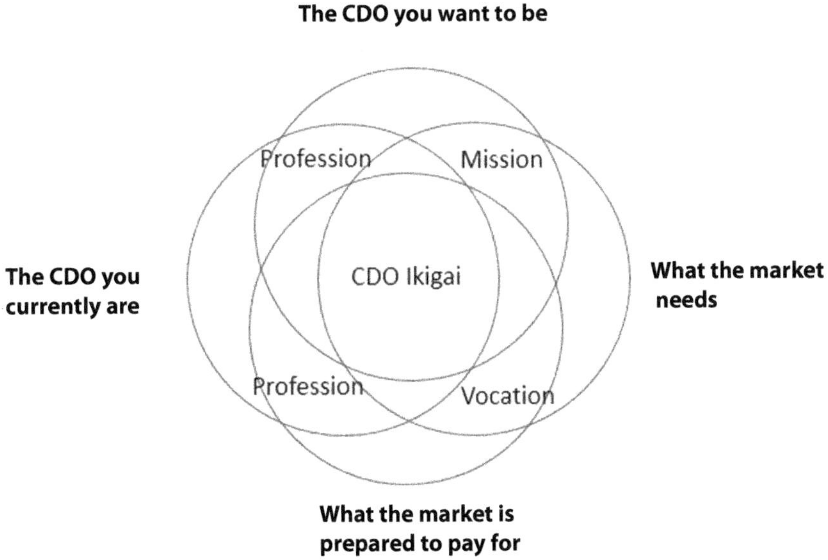

The CDO you want to be
Profession
Mission
The CDO you
currently are
CDO Ikigai
What the market
needs
Profession
Vocation
What the market is
prepared to pay for

Figure 14.2 *Ikigai for the CDO role*

more naturally an SCDO and you end up in a role that really requires an FCDO. Be honest with yourself: which CDO are you and which do you want to be? Once you have this clear in your mind, make sure that it is clear in the mind of any recruiter that you are working with and with any potential employer that you are talking to. Be aware that they may not really appreciate the difference between the two roles and types; you could be saving yourself and them a great deal of time and effort down the line.

Are you not currently a CDO, that's okay! What skills do you have that are part of the CDO skill set? What strengths do you have to lean on that move you in this direction?

If you are the type of CDO you want to be, then good for you! If you want to increase your skills, where do you want to take them? Are you a strong operational business leader who understands the value of data but needs to be more involved; or conversely, are you a strong technical leader but the business side is an area you need to explore more? Have you a strong analytical background and know that you need to understand the foundations better so as to look at the data more holistically? Is it worth getting a better handle of the data science side of the role if your skills are firmly rooted as an FCDO? Maybe for you it's about having a change of experience, working with a bigger organisation or an international one, or changing sectors. Maybe, like us, you want a different set of challenges.

If there is a gap, how are you doing to fill it? Remember the quote attributed to Lao Tzu: 'A journey of a thousand miles begins with a single step.' Any gap you want to fill will be filled only if you do something about it. Read a book, ask questions, take a course – but be proactive and take a positive step in the direction you want to go in. Ask yourself what's stopping you, and then find a way round, through, under or over it.

Let's be honest. You would hope that there would be a big overlap between what the market needs and what it is prepared to pay for, but unfortunately this is not always the case. For example, we have seen a surge in organisations wanting CDOs who can lead their AI capabilities and wrap machine learning through their core capabilities. That's all well and good, but in most cases they have no idea of the current quality of their data, and either no framework in place to understand that or a limited understanding of where the organisation faces real data risks, as well as a lack of cross-functional understanding of the value of data.

The only way you are going to understand either of these things is to do your market research. Check out what CDO roles are being advertised and keep track of them, review what skills are being asked for and what the role is supposed to achieve. Ask questions. Most recruiters and organisations are happy to answer questions, as they want to get the right candidate. There is no excuse for not doing your research.

For any specific role you are interested in applying for, make sure you research the business of your potential employer, or ask the right questions about the current level of data maturity in that organisation. Use what you discover to make your own assessment of the employer's needs: do they need an FCDO, or is the position more an SCDO role?

Alongside this, review your own skill set and strengths. Are you a data strategist with a full range of data skills, from data technology through data modelling and master data management to data governance, reporting, analytics and data science? Or are your skill set and strengths focused more in one area than another? The balance of your skills will help you to decide if you are an FCDO or an SCDO, but it will also help you to position your strengths into the business and to a recruiter.

It is best to be transparent about your strengths and the places where you feel that you aren't so strong: it will save everyone a lot of time and effort and will also add to your credibility in the market. Most of us have areas of strength, and other areas where we need to augment our team with skills that we aren't strong in - the interesting mix is what makes us human.

Remember that there is no point in trying to turn yourself into something that is alien to you, that doesn't resonate with your core values. As a person, it is important to be authentic, and as a CDO you will be leading people. You will struggle to pretend to be something that makes you uncomfortable, so please don't do it, for your sake and that of any future teams.

Here, Hilary McLennan, Organisational Behaviourist & Executive Coach who works with us on the CDO Summer School, describes authentic leadership:

What is authentic leadership?

Bill George[1] named five essential criteria for authentic leaders. Purpose, values, heart, relationships and self-discipline.

Building a conscious awareness of what those criteria contain for you personally can provide an important 'anchor' or 'touchstone' for the standards you commit to work to, the decisions you make and the relationships you build and maintain.

A word of warning, however! Our authentic self, while rooted in (what can sometimes be a stubborn) pride from past experiences and learning, also needs to maintain a future focus and motivation for growth and, yes, sometimes change.

Consciously balancing a candid self-awareness of why you are who you are, while demonstrating the curiosity and strength to move way out of your comfort zone and to learn and experiment, will undoubtedly feel uncomfortable at times. Just remember, it's usually when we are uncomfortable that we are learning the most.

Growing your authentic leadership identity for the future means having a sense of self that allows you to inquire, explore, understand and debate. The trick really lies in seeing real benefit in developing your authentic self in ways that aren't just a reflection of your past but a version of the best self you aspire to be.

Like any athlete training for performance, it takes time and consistency to reach and maintain your best performance.

Here are some tips to help you focus on how to train to be your best and most authentic self.

Understand your core personality profile

While we can't fundamentally change our personality, we can really benefit by having a deep self-awareness of how it drives and energises us. For instance, if you understand that you are extrovert you can consciously work and behave in an introvert way when required, but probably only for short periods of time. It can be tiring and demotivating!

Make the most of developing your emotional intelligence (EQ)

Not surprisingly, our emotions are likely to be closely connected to our authentic self because those five criteria matter to us!

The good news is that, if you choose to, you can develop your EQ throughout our adult life.[2] Developing our ability to notice, focus and choose the behaviours we want to demonstrate – even when under pressure – becomes much more likely when we have high EQ.

To fail fast, be aware of your self-critic

Many of the high achievers I coach are used to succeeding. Success is usually closely associated with knowing information both during education and career. The 'F' word of failing, whether fast or slow, is usually seen in black and white.[3] As a CDO you are likely to need to feel comfortable – even motivated by – ambiguity and innovation. Noticing partial successes and seeing failures as setbacks and challenges are ways of reframing what your self-critic may want you to pay attention to. Notice when your self-critical mantras are getting in the way of you learning and growing.

Sources

1 Bill George, *Authentic leadership: Rediscovering the secrets to creating lasting value*, 2004.

2 RocheMartin, *Emotional capital report, Technical manual*, 2016.

3 Steve Peters, *The chimp paradox*, 2012.

Remembering that the CDO is a business-lead role and not a technical one, you may need to adjust your profile to suit. Business owners and leaders will be looking for a range of skills and experience, regardless of their immediate pain points. Focus on your data skills, but make sure you have a balanced approach with both data and business skills. Take account of all of this in order to be the CDO that you can and want to be!

Preparing yourself for a CDO role

Unlike many other C-Suite roles, the CDO role doesn't yet have any form of professional qualification, standard or widely recognised professional body. Therefore it is very important to build up a visible and well-documented track record. If there is no CDO in your organisation, get involved in the CDO community and find a mentor. It is very difficult to jump straight from an IT, data governance or analytics role into being a CDO, so be prepared to do an 'apprenticeship'. Work alongside a CDO, be involved in the transformations, understand the strategy and expose yourself to the skill sets in which you are weak. Time in an 'apprenticeship' is time well spent and, again, will add to credibility. Inevitably you will see things fail – hopefully fast, with easy fixes; these failures will help you in the future and fast-track your work.

If you are coming from one of the wings into a CDO role make sure that you demonstrate a track record of leading and delivering transformation. A CDO, either FCDO or SCDO, will be heavily involved in transformation. Present yourself as an innovator/disruptor, but also a safe pair of hands capable of managing risk. And know which you are – an innovator or a disruptor – and demonstrate entrepreneurial behaviours.

We talk in Chapter 4 about needing to be a good storyteller. Well, that applies to you too. Be able to tell the story about why you are the right CDO for the organisation. That will also help when you actually get a role, as you will need to be able to sell the data vision, even if it is your predecessor's data strategy. You will need to be able to articulate the narrative of quite complex ideas in simple terms and relate the narrative to the business objectives. Think about the secret ingredients of the CDO (Chapter 4): relationship building, communications, credibility, passion for data, specialism, strategist and tactician and being lucky!

Another key piece of advice is to network and spend time with other CDOs; we are a friendly bunch and like to chat. The CDO community is still a relatively small one, albeit growing fast, and there are lots of events, webinars and podcasts to put you in touch with this community. Mix with them and listen and find your own opinions – we love adding new members into our mix. Really join in and bring your whole self along, share your opinions, as a fresh perspective is always welcome and might just set you apart within the growing profession of CDOs.

Finally, just start. Each journey starts with that first step; accept your trepidation and do it anyway. Good luck – not that we think you will need it!

15
The Chief Data Officer and the technology

Introduction

This chapter explores the tensions that may exist between data and IT, the boundary between IT and data, and the role of the CDO as a technology evangelist. The differences between 'information', 'digital' and 'data' are discussed, as well as the importance of shifting the conversation from 'systems' to 'data'.

Understand the context

> The biggest challenge a CDO will face is getting the IT department to be collaborative and accept that they don't own the data. They are far more likely to be defensive, controlling and resistant to change. They will have to play nicely for any data project to be a success.
>
> (Peter Ohlson, IT Delivery Manager, The Pensions Regulator)

This is an interesting topic, and so much will depend on a number of factors:

- the background, experience and technology expertise of the CDO
- the organisational structure that the CDO has been dropped into – do they report directly to the CTO/CIO, do they sit alongside these roles, or are they quite a long way from them reporting into Finance or the CFO or even the General Council?
- the state of the current technology estate
- the maturity of 'data' technology in the organisation
- ownership of business systems, e.g. the CRM or the asset management system
- the maturity of data ownership
- the data literacy of the leadership team.

Whatever the context, there are some common threads.

The CDO should have some 'data technology' understanding or, if not, recruit a senior colleague or partner to provide the cover. What 'data technologies' are we talking about? Without naming any individual brands or suppliers, the CDO, or someone close to them in their team, should be well versed in the 'art of the possible' in the technologies of master data management, metadata, data storage, data encryption, data lineage, reporting tools, dashboarding tools and analytics tools. But, this book isn't about these technical applications, it is to help the CDO, and perhaps the CTO, to understand the CDO's role and relationship to technology. It is also about understanding that some roles and responsibilities will shift and change. For example, the rapid development of low-code development environments is changing the size and structure of engineering teams.

The history of the social revolution

Let's look at a little bit of history:

> The first industrial revolution began in Britain in the late 18th century, with the mechanisation of the textile industry. Tasks previously done laboriously by hand in hundreds of weavers' cottages were brought

together in a single cotton mill, and the factory was born. The second industrial revolution came in the early 20th century, when Henry Ford mastered the moving assembly line and ushered in the age of mass production. The first two industrial revolutions made people richer and more urban. Now a third revolution is under way. Manufacturing is going digital.

Like all revolutions, this one will be disruptive. Digital technology has already rocked the media and retailing industries, just as cotton mills crushed hand looms and the Model T [Ford] put farriers out of work. Many people will look at the factories of the future and shudder. They will not be full of grimy machines manned by men in oily overalls. Many will be squeaky clean – and almost deserted.

> (*The Economist*, The third industrial revolution, Leader,
> 21 April 2012)

Look at how word processing, the (awful) spreadsheet and e-mail have changed the office; the amount of transformation has been amazing. So is 'data' a fourth industrial revolution, disrupting and transforming business? Uber and Air BnB are not taxi or hotel businesses, they are data businesses. There are many excellent case studies of more traditional businesses transforming their processes using data, sometimes in really dramatic ways. A fourth, data-driven industrial revolution may be under way, but what is really important is the emerging importance of data in the business as a driver for change, with the emphasis moving away from IT and technology. There is another angle to this: sometimes it is the 'state of data' within an organisation that is holding back transformation, and this needs to be addressed as a data problem, not as a technology problem. The days of business change being driven by advances in business technology are waning and business transformation is increasingly being driven by data.

An important factor in any data-related technology is the need for agility and timeliness – both key to being able to utilise data and get the value from it. It's all about how we move basic data into actionable insights, and doing that in a flexible way that feeds innovation. We do need to balance the systems that we have probably spent a lot of money on, and that have evolved as your organisation has grown to develop minimal viable products which allow you to try, test and learn quickly.

Who leads the technology?

It is interesting that many traditional IT departments have banks of SQL developers building databases, writing queries to bring data together and get data out of systems. The world has changed around them; the technologies being used by the data team, and even down in the front line of the business in many cases, have democratised the access to and usage of data. The new data technologies produce lines of code at a push of a button through a drag-and-drop visual interface. The analogy to the hand-weavers of the 17th century and the steam-powered looms of the 18th century is so obvious. Be mindful of the Luddites. These shifts cause tensions, and the ability to manage the tensions is based upon the secret ingredients of the CDO: credibility, communications and relationship building.

Inevitably, the CDO, or someone in the CDO's team, will be up to date with or even on the cutting edge of data technology. It may be that the existing IT team have been so busy maintaining and upgrading the existing systems that no one has the brief to review and assess new technologies and the business hasn't provided them with the criteria to assess against. This may be compounded by the role of the 'change function' and its method of operation in the organisation. If transformation and change is driven by the traditional route of the business defining its requirements – which is captured by business analysts and documented by project managers, and then the chosen system delivered by IT – who or what in the value chain is providing the cutting-edge suggestions about new and emerging technologies which meet the needs of the business? Who in the organisation knows about the modern, efficient tools for handling, transforming and presenting data, and who in that organisation knows about data?

CIOs have been saying for years that they want the business to define what it wants to achieve rather than what new, shiny system it wants installed, but have long lamented that everyone who has a PC believes they are an expert in IT. The truth is, CDOs aren't IT experts; we are experts in other fields, and the IT people have spent a great deal of time learning how to be experts in theirs. We've mentioned before that a great result comes when you bring different expertise together to create a better result than any individual can come up with on their own. Working with IT and technology is no different. It's great to have an understanding of the 'art of the possible'; you need to know what is available and how you can move towards your data nirvana, but you don't need to be an expert in IT.

When a shift takes place, such as a new CDO coming to the table, this can create tensions between 'traditional' IT departments and the (still relatively) new kids on the block – the data department. These tensions increase when IT becomes viewed as a 'service' provider, while business processes and transformation are being driven by data. However, by looking at what is really happening, i.e. everyone is really getting what they want, then you can overcome this. The CIO is getting the business direction, the business gets the outcome it wants – this is a great win-win situation.

The next problem is 'Where is the boundary between IT and data?' See Figure 15.1, and have a look at Chapter 8 and the bucket-and-water analogy. Basically, the CIO is responsible for the bucket and making sure it is in a safe place, has no holes in it and is the right size, and the CDO is responsible for the liquid in the bucket, where it comes from, what happens to it and the quality of it on its journey. There is no overlap unless the CIO is responsible for everything, and if that is the case, why have a CDO? Or perhaps the CTO and CDO report to the CIO or COO?

Data versus information

As a final problem, there tends to be confusion between the terms 'information', 'digital' and 'data'. We find this is a common problem. While the difference is clear to those of us who live and breathe the data world (and we have provided our understanding of the difference), it isn't so relevant to the rest of the organisation. Use language that makes them comfortable, and don't quibble over terminology, as long as you have the same understanding.

Information is derived from data, and data has to be mastered, managed, organised, stored and made available to be 'information' (Figure 15.1 on the next page). We often talk about a single piece of data being like a single piece of Lego: not terribly useful or exciting on its own, but put lots of different colours, sizes and shapes together and you can create amazing things. Information is data that has been collated, curated and contextualised, taking the raw and unprocessed data and giving it context to become information. The knowledge layer is where subject matter experts can use the data to create knowledge and make decisions, whereas wisdom takes data through to actionable insights used to create a body of wisdom to run the business. While Figure 15.1 implies that this is a linear process, the transition is anything but. Data doesn't sit in silos and will also flow back and forth (and jump) around the triangle.

So, while there is a clear distinction between information and data – one is derived from the other – you do have to remember that one person's information is another person's data. Information is not necessarily digital, but the confusion is that it may be digital, but digital isn't information. Now, are digital and data the same? The answer is no, in almost every case. In our book *Data Driven Business Transformation* we rename the 'information' layer of this pyramid. Instead of 'information' we term it 'collected, curated and contextualised data'. We believe that this provides a better understanding of what 'information' actually is, in the context, and avoids the confusion with the CIO. The DIKW (or DCCCKW) pyramid is a journey through data, not technology.

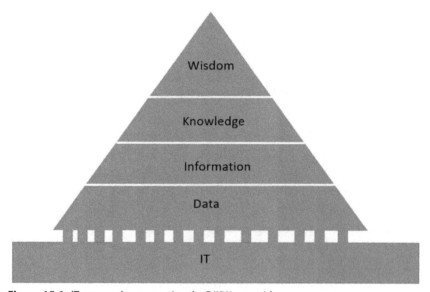

Figure 15.1 *IT as a service supporting the DIKW pyramid*

The words 'digital transformation' are still being used when in fact what they mean in many cases is data-driven transformation. Digital transformation is projects such as 'digital first': taking customers or the public from more traditional channels such as the phone, paper or even e-mail and driving them to a web-based or phone-based interface. This is done for three reasons: it is a better and quicker experience for the customer, it is cheaper for the supplier and the data is captured directly into the systems or database. That is digital transformation. When the organisation then starts to deliver tailored services or goods, or to profile the customer based on the data captured, this is data-driven transformation, not digital transformation. At an extreme, the digital interface is simply a way of capturing the data. It really all starts with the data.

16
The hoarding mentality and how to break it

Introduction

This chapter suggests that all organisations hoard data. It goes on to explore why we hoard data, where we store this data and the nature of 'dark data'. The chapter provides some suggestions for cutting through the hoarded data and the dark data and looks at the importance of counting the value of the data we do have.

The hoarding mentality

Have you ever watched those programmes on TV where a person is labelled a 'hoarder'? There tend to be various interviews with friends and family who are worried about the person and then pictures showing the person's home, which is usually so full of stuff that it is not fit to live in. You then see the person themselves, who sometimes recognises the problem, but not to the same extent that their nearest and dearest do. Normally they have found a way to make their home work as far as they are concerned: there are paths around the piles of things, as long as you pull in your stomach and walk sideways, and the oven makes a much better cupboard than it did a cooking implement, so cold food works just fine. If you watch them, though, you can tell that deep down they know that this isn't how most people live, but are in denial about the amount of time they are sitting in discomfort and working around a situation which, to outside eyes, could be easily solved. Most of us have tendencies in this direction: those shoes, tools or drawers full of bits that you keep just in case. Every single one of us must have experienced that feeling when you suddenly need something that you threw away the day before, because you had been storing it for so long and had never needed it, and so resolve to be more patient with your storage needs next time.

However, compulsive hoarding (which is what these individuals suffer from):

> ... is a pattern of behaviour characterised by excessive acquisition and an inability or unwillingness to discard large quantities of objects that cover the living areas of the home and cause significant distress or impairment. Compulsive hoarders may be aware of their irrational behaviour, but the emotional attachment to the hoarded objects far exceeds the motive to discard the items.
>
> ('Compulsive hoarding', *Wikipedia, the free encyclopedia*)

Compulsive hoarders have literally got to the point where it is more painful for them to throw something away than it is to live in a way that would make your eyes water. We are definitely not judging, and believe that you need to understand someone's life journey before passing any comment, so we wish anyone with this condition the help and support they need.

There are different therapies open to help people with this condition, but one of the more successful and recognised treatments for compulsive hoarding is cognitive-behavioural therapy (CBT), where the steps involved by the therapist may help the patient to:

- discover why they are compelled to hoard
- learn to organise possessions in order to decide what to discard
- develop decision-making skills
- declutter the home with a professional organiser
- have periodic visits and consultations to check a healthy lifestyle.

The CBT programmes which have been proved to be more effective are the ones that address the motivation of the sufferer and remove clutter with the person hoarding.

Data hoarding patterns

While not belittling an obviously serious condition, we would like to draw parallels with the companies we all work for. In this analogy, imagine your company is the house and your data is the stuff that is being hoarded, which makes all of us the hoarders. Does that bring a light-bulb moment for anyone? We all know that we keep too much data because we might need it: it's cheap to keep, so why not? We know that the amount of data we produce is growing exponentially, but what does that mean, what is our comparison and what value are we getting from all this data? The figure that tells us that 90% of data has been created in the last two years is widely known now, but what is more interesting is that if you took every book in every home, library and school they would account for only up to 6% of the data we currently hold – so what makes up the rest of it?! Until digital storage came into play, books and paper were how we stored all our knowledge. We're not sure in five years we will care what some stranger had for dinner but we'll bet it's stored somewhere in social media.

   We've also become conditioned to be lazy in this area. For years we have believed that IT will sort out all the digital stuff for us, like where and how things are stored, so we don't need to put any intelligence into it. Remember that really powerful Apple ad where the hammer was thrown through the screen, cracking the mundane world, freeing us to use all this great IT. Personal computers were smart, right? You could play chess against them and spreadsheets took all the hassle out of using a calculator. We are not for one second saying that the advent of the PC was not a good thing – far from it, we love the ability to grow, connect and feed our curiosity (we also have many fond memories of

Minesweeper, for those readers of a certain generation). What we are saying is that those spreadsheets didn't create themselves, we had to show the PC what we wanted it to do and be really clear about it, or you got some pretty odd findings; but somewhere down the line we forgot about our role in providing some of the intelligence in this equation. Not only did we let IT take the strain, but we started to abdicate our responsibilities completely when it came to making the decisions about data.

Also, why bother decluttering your data when you can store anything you want because it is cheap; and isn't bigger always better anyway? IT storage was always cheap, and it became cheaper and cheaper as we improved it and generated more, so volume became a consideration. It almost became a badge of honour to say how much data your organisation was storing. We created new storage systems and took all the out-of-date documents from our old systems, which we had filled till they fell over, and crammed them all into our new, shiny, work-of-art software because it was easier to lift and shift than to apply a level of intelligence to what we actually needed, wanted or would ever use again. If you couldn't find it in the first place, how does moving it make it any better? If you pick up a boxful of snakes and put them into a different box, guess what? You still have a box of snakes, it's just now they are in a bigger box with gold plating on it.

And this is before we get started on the big data agenda. Bigger does not equal better, and, as with so many things in life, it's what you do with it that counts. Yes, we can do some absolutely brilliant things with data; our unicorns can be unleashed and come up with those flashes of brilliance. They probably aren't coming up with those flashes of brilliance based on 47 copies of the same photo that you e-mailed to your friends while you were on holiday to make them envious of your tan lines. They are also not achieving them based on the fact that, because you didn't trust your IT, you have copied that precious document onto your C drive and onto a shared drive, sent it to yourself so you have e-mail as a back-up, and created a copy on a flash drive stored in the back of your cupboard, all before we even talk about the weakness and lack of logic behind many enterprise storage solutions.

Even when or if we recognise that it is something we should be doing with our data, we suffer from the 'I'll get around to that' syndrome. It hasn't been urgent and there is always something more pressing to be done, so it gets put to the back of the drawer and we get to it later (you know, that magic drawer full of the stuff that you promise yourself you will get around to, which mysteriously grows over time into a full-blown set of drawers or cupboard - you know we all have one!) The organisational equivalent to this is an example used above: we copied all that junk and contaminated our nice new system because organising the data wasn't the most pressing, urgent problem we had at the time. Let's be honest with ourselves - it takes time and money to think about organising data and build schemas, and there is normally something else we prefer to spend the time and money on. Reactiveness is just a normal part of everyday life in a business, and we're definitely not casting aspersions on people who have had to make tough budgetary and strategic decisions - we've made them ourselves and, with hindsight, would have to question, if we could go back in time, whether we would make different ones.

It's even harder to get rid of something if no one will take ownership of it! Information flows through our organisations; it really is their lifeblood. Different parts of your company use the same information in different ways; your information isn't static and it changes and morphs as it journeys through your company. No one wants to take ownership of the information/data because they sit in silos and, while it enters their silo, it also leaves. Why would they take responsibility for something they have no control over? What if they make a decision about the management of the data, such as deletion, and it was the wrong decision? It's much safer to keep it 'just in case' than to take the risk of deleting it and then finding it was critical to someone else in the business. The problem is this: if you can't find owners for your information, then how can you ever ask them?

This is partially how we have ended up in this mess in the first place. No one wants to be responsible for deleting data that proves to be incredibly valuable, never mind a whole system full of the stuff. (This is where the difference between data and information, as discussed in Chapter 15, comes in.) It isn't that all of a sudden being a CDO means you make all these decisions about what is and isn't valuable. How could you completely understand every part of the business and take on all of that responsibility? You would really be setting yourself up to fail. Rather, what you bring with you - the information architecture, the data domain owners, rigorous policies so you know what to delete or achieve – is what brings the understanding. So, while you don't make the decisions, you do know who will.

We have both taken it upon ourselves to stop swathes of reports over our careers – reports that looked repetitive, inconsistent and living nightmares, to be honest – but every attempt to ask if people wanted them was met with fierce assertions that they were completely and totally necessary. It turns out that we were taking the wrong approach. Instead of asking, we took the report away and waited to see who missed it. In this way we identified who really did need the information and what was it they really wanted.

The reports aren't the only problem. Most organisations hoard data in hidden caches. This is 'dark data', stored in endless spreadsheets and Microsoft Access databases. People are storing it, but how much use are they really getting from it? We're sure that the person using it thinks they are holding on to some priceless treasure, but, even before you take into account all the manipulation that they put into it, is it really worth the effort?

Finally, there is the old favourite – all that duplicated data. Those situations where someone has created a document, sent it to someone for a review and that person also saved a copy and sends it back, which gets saved again with some random number of a version because the person saving it has forgotten how many people they have asked to review it and how many have come back. None of which get deleted. The business probably also has a huge store of e-mails, and e-mails with attachments, which are probably already stored by the sender and then are saved by the recipient, who also retains the e-mail with the attachment. Then, of course, there are the situations where the e-mail is saved with the attachment, and the attachment is saved and printed off and retained as a hard copy. This doesn't even include data held in development, test, user acceptance testing, pre-production systems and back-ups. The list is endless, and most of it at best is worthless and at worst could be damaging, because it stops you finding that little nugget of gold you are really after. None of it would be retained if the organisation had functional archiving, deletion and version control policies.

Google are rumoured to store over 10 exabytes of data (that's 10 billion gigabytes); or, to put it another way, a gigabyte is about 1,600 books or 9 metres of books stacked side to side, so that's 90 billion metres' worth of books that Google alone holds. Then you've got Facebook, Amazon and Microsoft, to name a few other heavy data storage companies. Experts now predict that over 40 zettabytes of data will be stored by 2020. That's a lot of data. There are many absolutely brilliant uses of data in our everyday life - checking directions on our phones, predicting epidemic outbreaks or streamlining the flow of traffic through towns - but that's still a lot of data.

Bringing us back to our businesses, how do we cope with this abundance of information? The truth is, we don't. It doesn't matter that if we can't find what we want we just create more. It's as if we are feeding an endlessly hungry machine that devours all our data, constantly shovelling in fact after fact. But what do we get for our effort? Why do we feed the beast? Our storage systems are just like the woodshed we have in our garden. We know the exact piece of wood we want is in there, we are completely sure of it; now, do we (a) search through the massive pile of bits of wood that we swear must reproduce on their own because we never put all of that in there, or do we (b) go out and buy it again and then subsequently end up sticking something else in the pile? We think you can figure that one out.

Instinctively, we know we can't store everything but are reluctant to throw anything away. What if we find out that we needed that piece of data after we no longer had it? How foolish would that make us look? We would have to spend more money and time gathering the data again, when it must be easier just to keep it all in the first place. Fear is a powerful motivation for organisational paralysis, but yielding to it is pretty inexcusable.

For the alternative argument, what if we have data retention policies but they are not reflective of the needs of the organisation? When the wrong policies are in place you end up driving the wrong behaviour. Anything with property data or asset data, for instance, can have a long lifetime. However, if you haven't worked out your information architecture yet, how do you define what lifetime each domain has? We've worked in organisations where, because the policy was wrong (i.e. didn't account for some extremely long timescales for data retention), people who looked after that particular type of data put it on flash drives, storage drives, C drives - all of which contravened other organisational policies - because they had to, yet it had never occurred to them to fix the policy which was incorrect in the first place. These people were just trying desperately to do the right thing, but doing it in the wrong way because they just couldn't see any other option.

We've also worked with organisations that very proudly showed us their nice, shiny data retention policy that said everything must be deleted after two years. By now you might have a guess about what we think about this one-size-fits-all type of policy. They had paid no attention to the different types of data they looked after, and the result was keeping some things longer than they needed to and throwing out others before they could probably assess the impact of losing them. The very worst thing was that they were living in denial; they thought they had it all sorted, and so weren't paying any more attention to it. We would rather be knowingly wrong than delusionally right; at least we would then still be thinking about the problem and how to put a solution in place.

To go back to our starting point, we have become like the hoarders who plot little pathways through an overcrowded house and, while we recognise that it's not the best way to treat all of this stuff, we don't recognise the overall harm we are doing to ourselves and our company. As long as we can get from A to B or are dimly aware of where our kitchen or bedroom is supposed to be we are kidding ourselves that we are doing okay, even though, deep down, we all know we aren't.

Breaking the patterns

It's not all doom and gloom, however. Help is at hand, but we are suggesting that we all need a healthy dose of therapy. Using this analogy, let's go back to look at the steps that can help us. If we invented a data therapist to work with us they would help us to:

1   Discover why we are compelled to hoard. Do your investigation on what is really happening within your organisation, what is your root-cause analysis? What is broken and driving the organisation to come up with work-arounds? Human beings are great at following the path of least resistance, so if they are working around something there will be a reason. Having your information architecture for this will help you, even if you are just at the highest conceptual level, as it gives you terminology to use

that your business should recognise (if it doesn't, then your model is wrong; you might want to try that again).

2   Learn to organise possessions in order to decide what to discard. Get your policies and guidance right. What is your data retention policy? What does it cover? Does it manage to cope with different types of data? Do you understand the value of what you have (more on this below) and do you understand the risks associated with it?

3   Develop decision-making skills. Hone your prioritisation skills as a company, understand what you are trying to achieve as a business and how the data you store and the information you use will help you achieve that. If it doesn't, then you need to ask yourself why you are keeping it. Utilising the technology to help you can be a great enabler here. Forcing you to think about how long you need to keep something is a great start; a whole-scale categorisation of a data domain is again a good starting point, but not a complete substitute for the experts who understand the data, why they need it and what they are going to use it for, and so really think about it.

4   Declutter the home with a professional organiser. There are some areas where you just need an expert to help you. Just ask a teenage boy: he will tidy his room with a great deal more motivation and efficiency when his mum is standing over him holding the power cable to his Xbox while expertly informing him what their next task should be than when he is left to his own devices. There are tools to help you get rid of your clutter, there are companies specialising in nothing but cleaning your data estate, and sometimes it's just easier for someone else to rip the Band-Aid off – once you are sure you have set the right rules for them to follow!

5   Gain and perform relaxation skills (we just left this one in because we liked it). Everyone needs to relax and gain a bit of perspective once in a while. The company has to run, otherwise you have no business; you are there to support them, not to stop them doing anything, but you will be of no use to anyone if you drown yourself in e-mails. Take a walk around the block once in a while to remember why you are doing this.

6   Have periodic visits and consultations to check you are operating a healthy lifestyle. Do your assurance: all policies need to be checked and potentially updated, all areas can take their eye off the ball occasionally. There is no point in doing what will feel like a lot of painful work to make your landscape look pretty if you don't put the effort in to keep it that way. Have you seen how quickly your garden can become overgrown in summer? Your data, similarly, wants to be in that uncontrolled state so that it can grow faster.

> Balancing the ad hoc work and tools of data discovery, that in many cases is led by the line of business, with the requirement for rationalised and centralised business intelligence, mostly led by IT, is one of the biggest challenges faced by organisations on the journey to becoming data-driven businesses.
>
> (Sebastian Darrington, Managing Director, Exasol, UK)

Finally, this will all work best for you if you make sure that you tackle the following two things. First, focus on the whys and not just the whats: why is your organisation storing everything? Why do your people store things on their flash drives? And why haven't you updated your policies in ten years? This helps you to stay away from the blame game, which does not help anyone, and gives you some understanding of how you can stop it happening again, or it might let you find out something you missed.

Second, work with your organisation to understand it and help to change it. No one likes feeling that changes are being imposed on them, and you probably aren't the expert in every single area of your business. Let them do what they are good at and you do what you are good at. Give them credit for all the expertise they bring to the process and help them to understand why you are doing what you are doing. We have learned that people are much more motivated to change if they genuinely understand why they are being asked to modify their behaviour and can see the benefits of doing so.

Remember, data hoarding is only one of the areas that you need to fix as a CDO, but it is a very important one, especially for the FCDO. By getting rid of what you don't need, use or want, you can make quick wins with your IT department because you have just saved them money, while at the same time making the data you already have much more accessible, utilising exactly the same tools the organisation has already invested in. If you can produce that kind of success within a company, you can buy yourself some wiggle room to focus on the enterprise-wide transformation that will give you the big changes.

> Having sat through many presentations from government organisations, I agree with your comments around not collecting/hoarding data for the sake of it. Data should be seen as an asset and not a chore, it needs to be exploited, and so the focus should be on outcomes and should be measured on the value the outcomes bring.
>
> (Dave Cull, Central Government Account Executive)

Understanding the value of what you have

More and more work is being done on trying to define the value of data within an organisation. What that means for you will differ considerably depending on what type of organisation you are in and whether you are an FCDO, SCDO or even TCDO, but what will stay the same is that you will need to look at the different aspects of what comprises the importance of data and information in order to come up with the right answer for your company.

Right at the beginning of your journey you need to articulate that data has a value, even when you have no idea what that value might be. Getting the organisation to treat its information as a company asset in the same way it would any other company asset is the first hurdle you will face in this area. This is an intangible asset, which makes it really difficult to articulate as an asset, but you would suffer as an organisation if you didn't have it - ask any company that has lost data and they will happily tell you about the pain that it causes. If data didn't have a value it wouldn't cause a problem if you didn't have it - would it?

Why would you even care about understanding what value it has? Because, if you understand how valuable your data and information is to your company, you can look after it appropriately. Getting resources to look after the crown jewels is pretty easy - they are worth a lot of money, people would likely take them if it was easy, so it is probably best to look after them and protect them. Is the case of looking after a folder full of paper quite so easy? Probably not, unless you understand what is in the folder. Now, what if we told you the folder was full of the cures for cancer – its value now depends on how much you care about looking after that piece of information and the appropriate action to protect it. In this area, it all depends on context.

To be able to understand the value for your company you need to look at the different factors that give your data its value:

- Are you the only company that has it?
- How accurate is it?
- How complete is it?
- Is it up to date?
- How relevant is it?
- What are you using it for?
- Can you use it for more than you currently use it for?
- What would happen if you lost it?

> Very well thought out and articulated. The immediate strategy is also critical as that is where most resistance will be around and as a result most of the efforts. If you can successfully make a case for getting rid of or managing the silos better and everything else that are counterproductive to the CDO journey, a future where businesses can realise the benefits and have a true data asset awaits.
>
> (Prakash Baskar, CxO advisor, strategy, governance, data and analytics, business-technology leader and author)

As every organisation is different, only you can envision how these factors play into how you understand the value of your data in your company, but understanding these factors can help you when you build your strategy, and when you convey your data story with evidence. It gives you somewhere to turn when you have the inevitable conversations about 'Why should we invest in this area?' or 'Why do you want money for a project team?' It is imperative that you can sell your vision, paint your picture with words and take people on a journey; without any form of evidence you will struggle to get off the starting blocks. Whether that evidence is risk based (i.e. how much threat you are under or how much you could save by preventing something possibly happening) or value based (the positive side of the equation, where you can use your insights for something really special), it is up to the maturity of your organisation on your data journey.

> [N]ot only I totally agree to your approach, we put it in practice in my compañía and it works.
>
> (Mariola Lobato, Data Quality, Data Governance
> and Digital Transformation Director)

17
Data and information ethics

Introduction

This chapter stresses the importance of 'making sure you think before you do'. Data is dangerous, it is combustible and should be handled with caution. The theory of unintended consequences is also explored.

The need for customer data ethics arises from two factors – concentrated market power of a few digital tech giants controlling massive amounts of customer data and consumers' deep seated concerns about how their data is collected and used.

(Mike McGuire, Vice President Analyst in Gartner's marketing practice)

Opportunities and ethics

There's a common saying in the UK along the lines of 'just because you can doesn't mean you should', usually said to someone who is using their money, skills or power in a way that isn't morally the best. Pulling our company's data together, governing it and making it trustworthy and then capitalising on it for the good of our organisation could give us a tremendous amount of power – so how do we intend to use it? Irrespective of how ethical our intentions are, what about the unintended consequences?

Advances in data and how we use it can and have provided us with huge opportunities to improve our public and private lives. This, coupled with the gradual reduction in human oversight and the growing awareness among the public about the use of data in their everyday lives means these opportunities come at a price: the increasingly significant ethical challenges we face in this area. It's important to find the balance between allowing and even encouraging innovation and facing some really regrettable consequences. We need to be able to build on data, share and collaborate, but to do so in an ethical and sustainable fashion.

Regulation and legislation has also become much more aware of the consequences of the misuse of data; and legal measures around data protection, intellectual property, data storage, anti-discrimination and confidential information all strive to tackle areas where data meets ethical concerns.

A definition of data ethics was formulated by Luciano Floridi and Maricrosaria Toddeo for the Royal Society in late 2016:

> the branch of ethics that studies and evaluates moral problems related to data (including generation, recording, curation, processing, dissemination, sharing and use), algorithm (including artificial intelligence, artificial agents, machine learning and robots) and corresponding practices (including responsible innovation, programming, hacking and professional codes), in order to formulate and support morally good solutions (e.g. right conducts or right values).

While this is a very detailed statement and brilliant for scholars, we think that the Open Data Institute's rather more straightforward definition is more in line with our idea of trying to keep the idea of data accessible:

> Branch of ethics that evaluates data practices with the potential to adversely impact on people and society – in data collection, sharing and use.

Data ethics is about the responsible and sustainable uses of data, and should align to the organisation's compliance and responsible business practices. Responsible business practices are often challenged, and there are often very obvious examples of big corporations not being responsible, especially with data; in these cases we can clearly see a lack of 'data ethics'. The use of data must be fair, open and deliver non-discriminatory outcomes. History has been littered, even modern history, like yesterday, with people and organisations using data to discriminate. Data can be a force for good and can highlight and identify discrimination.

If you wish to bundle up the 'why' case for data ethics for senior management, it may look like this:

> Corporate values, unfair bias and privacy. There are many examples of organisations letting down their customers with poor data ethics in one of these three spaces.

The dilemmas of data ethics

There are so many areas of data where we need to think about ethical considerations: how it is generated, recorded or shared – that's before you get into the ethics of AI and machine learning interpreting data. Overlay that with the idea that people could deliberately misuse data, and you have a great deal of potential for non-ethical things to happen. Add in the dimension of differing global behaviours when it comes to ethics, differing values, political and social behaviours, and then you already have a minefield when it comes to data ethics, even before you consider whether differing attitudes to data ethics across countries affects companies' competitive advantage.

There are many different examples of where data can tell us things that others may not be aware of. Our supermarkets, for instance, could tell if we are at risk of developing diabetes through the change in our shopping patterns – how open would customers be to being told that? What if your local supermarket told you that, with enough warning for you to do something about it and avoid the illness in the first place? Do you think they would be thanked, or lose a customer because no one wants to feel snooped on? Using this as an example of a larger issue, diabetes costs the National Health Service in the UK about £1 billion per year, and surely prevention is better than the cure, so should the government work with the supermarkets to identify early warning signs and target people directly, and how would that make those people feel?

In subtle (and not so subtle) ways our lives are changing. TV shows us adverts that are tailored to the demographics within our households (knowing this, we sometimes do sit and wonder what information the advertisers have on us to push some of the adverts our way!), and we discuss incredibly private items on social media, broadcasting our every thought and whim in a way that would have been unheard of even 20 years ago.

A major consideration in data ethics is how easy it is to disadvantage someone or a group of people either on purpose or through bias in the data, which is just too easy to do. Look at the research paper 'The Geography of Pokémon GO: Beneficial and Problematic Effects on Places and Movement' by Ashley Colley et al whose 'results also strongly suggest that the geographic distribution of PokéStops substantially advantages areas with large white (non-Hispanic) populations.' Because the game advantages urban areas. I doubt (and hope) that this bias wasn't intentional however it's a clear demonstration of unintended consequences.

Omission of data can have ethical considerations. Especially as data may not have been collected in the past in a way that we would now want to use it.

One of the most important things to say about the gender data gap is that it is not generally malicious, or even deliberate. Quite the opposite. It is simply the product of a way of thinking that has been around for millennia and is therefore a kind of *not* thinking. A double not thinking, even: men go without saying, and women don't get said at all. Because when we say human, on the whole, we mean man.

(Caroline Criado Perez, Invisible Women:
Exposing Data Bias in a World Designed for Men)

Transparency and fairness, terms and conditions need to be simpler and clearer.

Making ethical mistakes can have a big impact on the future of how we treat data. If we get it wrong, public perception can change really quickly and have a very negative impact on what we can do; laws can change and enforce compliance, but as the use of data evolves at such a fast pace, will the legislation cover what it needs to? In some ways we are already trying to deal with this problem at the legislative level, but are we addressing the core problems we are trying to fix or are we constraining ourselves too much? And is this the price we are paying for not taking this area and its security seriously enough? Yet we have to progress, that is inevitable; stagnation serves no purpose, so how do we innovate responsibly?

What's interesting is that while we are moving towards clear definitions on data ethics, we aren't collaborating as much as we would like to. There are many organisations involved in the debate around data ethics and striving to help make the murky picture a little bit clearer, with guidance such as:

- the UK government's Data Ethics Framework (June 2018)
- the European Commission's Data protection and privacy ethical guidelines (2009)
- UK National Statistician's Data Ethics Advisory Committee's Ethical Principles
- The US Farm Bureau's Privacy and Security Principles for Farm Data (2016),

among others. We want to give you an idea that while this is still an area that we don't feel we have 'got right', it is one where a great deal of thoughtful work is being progressed, so when you are facing your own ethical dilemmas or thinking about taking greater advantage of your data please don't start from scratch. Review what is out there; build and collaborate so that we constructively challenge each other to get better.

In fact, a really good starting point if you are about to undertake a new data project is the Data Ethics Canvas from the Open Data Institute. It has been developed to identify and manage ethical issues at the start of a project that uses data. We like this one in particular, as it has people as its core consideration, but it is not all encompassing, so you do need to continue to challenge yourselves.

Striking a balance between the innovation and advancement in this area with protection of privacy and human rights will be difficult, but not impossible. It is important that we consider this as part of what we do. Everyone needs to find their own ethical standpoint; we aren't here to preach but to raise awareness of the issue, so that whatever you choose to do, you do it consciously. This can be a difficult one, but we not only need to think through the direct consequences of our actions but also the unintended consequences. Putting out open data sets that individually are easily classified as open is one thing, but what about the data aggregation effect? Once you put it all back together, what if you end up exposing something completely top secret that could cause harm?

The first step is to understand the role we play in all of this and to take responsibility for it. Ask yourself some questions about the impact of what you are intending (a simple test would be 'would you be happy to tell people what you had done?'). Think through the consequences as much as possible, both the direct and the unintended ones, and then monitor for the reaction to it. Have you been not only lawful in your thinking but fair? Are you clear and transparent about what you are intending and how you describe it? Looking for your unknown unknowns is a really difficult position to be in, but if you don't look you will probably never see them. At least monitoring what is happening gives you that fighting chance.

> **The strength of a nation derives from the integrity of the home.**
>
> (Confucius)

As well as the actions you take, you also have to consider how you will share what you are doing with your organisation. It is important to be clear on your approach to data and the ethical use of data. Make sure that your approach is documented and actively shared. Data ethics is a team sport.

Alignment between ethics and values is another dimension; being clear and transparent with employees provides clarity and prevents rogue behaviour.

We need to think about data ethics across the data value chain: data sourcing, data algorithms (processing) and data practices. A framework across the data value chain could have four elements:

- **Principles**. What are you trying to achieve with data ethics? Much of this has been covered above.
- **Ethical assessment**. These are the questions that each part of the business should be asking itself when using data, or proposing to use data. These questions could be built into the existing project or governance frameworks.
- **Accountabilities.** Who is responsible for data ethics in the organisation? Who will call out and challenge the non-ethical use of data? In a data mature organisation you would really hope that everyone felt empowered to do this. If your organisation isn't at that point yet, then perhaps data ethics could become part of the 'whistle-blower' mandate.
- **Guide rails** to ensure that people have a framework within which to operate freely. Ultimately, it may be possible to have a Data Ethics Charter which is publicised both internally and externally. Some organisations are creating Data Ethics Councils. It is even possible to create templates in a similar way for a Data Privacy Impact Assessment to assess the ethical use of data. In many cases it makes sense to merge these two together so as to not over-burden the business.

Ultimately, you have to take action. This is an evolving field, so don't be afraid to admit it if things didn't go the way you wanted them to and you need to course-correct.

18
The Chief Data Officer and data governance

Introduction

This chapter explains how data governance can help and not hinder the business; in fact, how data governance can drive innovation. The elements of good data governance are outlined, and how good data assurance can keep the data strategy and business on track.

Data governance and data protection

Data governance is one of the pillars of a data strategy and a large part of the CDO's task and responsibilities. Why are we singling out data governance in particular for its own chapter in this book, and not master data management, metadata or some other core deliverable in a data strategy?

The answer is twofold. First, it could be argued that data governance is the underpinning principle of any data capability: it is fundamental to the work of a CDO. Second, the introduction of GDPR in May 2018 brought data governance into sharp focus, and the role of the Data Protection Officer (DPO) within organisations is worth some examination in relation to the CDO; as the legislation has become more embedded, so the role has evolved and become more understood. So, the first reason for examining the CDO's role in data governance is the importance of the business outcomes that effective data governance provides and the second reason is regulatory pressures.

In fact, since the first edition of this book more countries are taking the regulation of data protection much more seriously. Various African nations have introduced (or are reviewing) amendments to their 2004 law on the protection of personal data which strengthen the rights of the individual with regard to their data. US states such as California, with 'the California Consumer Privacy Act', seek to establish an enforceable right of privacy. Canada has also reviewed and changed some of its privacy regulations, and the list goes on.

Not only have regulations been updated (and tightened) but they are also, in our opinion, being taken much more seriously. Equifax agreed to pay a fine of $575 million because not only did they fail to fix a critical vulnerability months after a patch had been issued, but they then failed to inform the public of the breach for weeks after it had been discovered. Let's be honest, anyone can make a mistake, but that was a big one. They didn't own up to it, and wow, did they pay for it!

Before we look at what data governance is, let's think about what it's not, because it is one of the most misunderstood parts of data. We've seen so many companies describe their MDM (master data management) or data quality product as data governance. You can't slap a label on your catalogue and lineage capabilities and think you've 'done' governance. It's also not purely about data privacy, but it is a big helper. Having a central repository for your data doesn't solve all your governance problems. We understand that, because it's moving you away from your siloed thinking, it can help; but again, it's not data governance. It is absolutely not an IT programme, nor is it a project that has an end, after which you get to put it back into its little box and congratulate yourself.

Most importantly - it's not boring! In fact, we increasingly think it's a game changer when done well.

Data governance (DG) refers to the overall management of the availability, usability, integrity, and security of the **data** employed in an enterprise. A sound **data governance** program includes a governing body or council, a defined set of procedures, and a plan to execute those procedures.

(Margaret Rouse, definition from www.WhatIs.com)

Data governance is first and foremost a business initiative. Data must be made available to the business; there is no benefit in locking data up so that the business cannot use it. Locking data up may not be intentional; it may be a function of relationships with partners who effectively charge your organisation to access their own data. Data must be usable, it must be mastered and in a format that can be used by the business. Too many organisations spend 80% of their time and effort sorting data out and only 20% of their time and effort looking at the insight revealed by the data. This balance needs to be reversed to become 20:80 on time versus insight. The data must have integrity; we must assess, understand and maintain the data quality and integrity. Good decisions can be made only from good data. Finally, the security of the data is paramount for good business outcomes. In simple terms, the business cannot afford to lose its data, its asset. If an organisation, the business, can't access its data, or doesn't understand its data, or even worse doesn't trust its data, then effectively it has 'lost' its data. It has squandered an asset, and that could be costly and risky.

Various aspects of availability, usability, integrity and security are also important to data regulation compliance. The CDO is not and should not be the DPO. Data protection generally relates to a subset of the data used across an organisation and is only one dimension of data that needs to be considered by the CDO. The CDO must balance value and risk delivery, whereas the role of the DPO is to ensure regulatory compliance and is focused on risk reduction more than on value release. If an organisation has appointed a DPO or Senior Information Risk Officer (SIRO), then this role should be independent of the CDO. However, the DPO will rely on the CDO to provide assurance and evidence of compliance with GDPR, and this assurance should be one of the outcomes of data governance.

It is easy to understand that data governance is a fundamental pillar of the CDO's data capability. As a result, an early delivery from an

FCDO could be an enterprise data governance framework. In simple terms, the CDO's office will run the enterprise data governance group (EDGG) and each business unit will have its own subordinate data governance group (DGG) which reports back to the EDGG and implements the policies and framework of data governance developed by the EDGG.

This has to fit into your wider organisation and operating model. If this language or way of working is alien to how you normally run your organisation, then modify it to something that resonates better. Good data governance has to be part of the normal governance of the organisation, not a bolt-on.

But remember that, with governance especially, no one size fits all. You need to understand and embed the goldilocks level of governance for your organisation. Not too soft, not too hard, just right. We can cover the key elements that you need to think about, but you really need to make sure that it works for your organisation. Over time it can seem like governance is just stopping you from doing things, and that's where governance gets a bad name. You aren't governing data for the sake of it but, rather, to make sure that you are striking a balance between sustainability and innovation.

Enablement, not red tape

> Don't start with the infrastructure or the technology, start with the projects. Think of yourself as an enabler much more than an owner, and concentrate on making the organisation smarter.
>
> (Marco Bressan, Chief Data Scientist, BBVA)

Now we are assuming, since you are reading this, that you are a bit of a data geek, or at the very least interested in data and ready to understand that it is critical to how an organisation works. So data is the be all and end all . . . well, not quite. You may be totally passionate about this, but there are ways and means to convey that passion that bring people on the journey with you. Locking people down so that they cannot do anything other than what you dictate to them probably isn't going to win you those hearts and minds that you really need in order to do this role well.

Governance doesn't only have to be about control, it can (and should) be about enabling the organisation to move forward. Having the business in control of its own governance doesn't have to equal chaos. Equally, just because something is operated in the business doesn't mean that it is not governed. Let's be honest, though; we're not saying governance isn't based upon control elements – of course it is, you are laying out the direction you want people to head in and giving them ways of getting there – but what we *are* saying is that it is also about enablement. You are freeing the organisation from the tyranny of poor data governance and removing the shackles of repetition. Okay, maybe we are going a little far, but you are enabling them to operate in an environment where they can trust their data and information. You are enabling them to focus on what is important to them and you should be agile enough to cope with the flex the company needs in order to be comfortable, or at least healthily uncomfortable.

Too many times we have heard that 'it would be easier without customers', but just remember that you wouldn't have a business without customers, whether they are internal or external. We aren't dictators, but if we are not careful in any governance role it's easy to come across that way. We are here to help the business, not to stop them doing anything; we can be a bit over-protective sometimes, over-zealous, and just because we mean well does not mean we don't have the potential to harm the business. By putting the control into the hands of the business you have an army of willing volunteers all pulling in the same direction: you don't give up control, but you enable it, supporting self-governance and encouraging the data passion to spread.

This subject, like so many others in life, is about balance. While you need to make sure that the company are coming with you on your wonderful data journey and that they don't stray too far from the lovely, safe path you have laid out for them, you also have to let them do their job, growing and learning at the same time. While you lay out your grand plans and set up your stall for great data governance, putting in place the wonderful policies you might need to over-control for a time while the organisation gets used to operating in a different manner, that must be accompanied by help, support and the understanding that this might not be a comfortable path for everyone. This isn't about embracing either extreme but letting the company find the right level of control and governance. Like every pendulum, it will swing back; the trick is to get the pendulum of control into a comfortable place which allows the company to operate easily and happily, while providing the comfort blanket they need that reassures them they are getting the best from their data. You will need to consider, is there a risk to quality if you trust the company?

The purpose of data governance

To put some flesh on the bones: the purpose of data governance is to enable co-ordinated initiatives which improve the reliability of data and insight across the enterprise; to (at a minimum) establish a common approach; in larger organisations leaning towards a more centralised approach to establish and maintain a common set of data definitions that are used to ensure consistency of data and enforcing an agreed set of centralised data management processes for managing the development and ongoing maintenance of data and reports.

The key components of data governance are:

- **policies** - defined by the EDGG to outline the key ways to work with data and deliver insight
- **processes** - details of how the principles and policies will be applied and enforced
- **organisational design** - assignment of ownership of data and responsibility for data
- **data architecture and design** - articulation of location, lineage and relationships for key data
- **technology** - the tools required to manage data and provide the standardised reporting.

But, as with much in life, it is what you do with them that counts. How do all your elements of data governance fit together, working seamlessly to make data governance fit with the organisation, not clash with it. You can have all of these to a more or less degree, depending on what your organisation is doing with its data (financial institutions tend to have heavier governance, for example), but you do need to document it so that you understand and are making conscious decisions about your data governance and not just letting the tide take you.

A data governance framework as outlined above will meet both the business and compliance outcomes that are required.

> [The] biggest topic emerging CDOs deal with is the clarity of ownership of data – be it reference data, master data, transaction data or structural or classification or functional BIAs data with IP rights . . . the list is vast and complex! The already thin and blurred lines between business, IT, including cloud/SaS providers and ultimately end customers, is getting more and more dotted, especially due to new digital transformation with added flavours of interfacing the most complex and slow-changing ERPs. Industry is still trying to figure out data risks vis-à-vis process accountability fighting with business risk and compliance/legal aspects. Across most of the industries, 'Who really owns and is accountable for data?' is becoming the iceberg question – most of which is only partly answered with scientific matrices in the realm of advancements in disruptive innovations.
>
> (Dhiraj Deo, an experienced cross-functional business transformation professional)

The principles of data governance are simple and you should feel free to assess these as fit for purpose for your organisation:

- consistency of data without unnecessary duplication
- quality which is proactively assessed and standards
- ownership and accountability defined across the data life cycle and recorded data catalogues
- business alignment which ensures that data is regarded and treated as a key business asset
- access to relevant users, kept secure through access control without locking data down for no purpose
- providing trusted insight.

We've covered the roles and responsibilities in Chapter 10 on teams, but you should be able to draw which team and organisation roles are critical to data governance, such as the data steward and data champion, and identify where in your operating model they are working.

An important part of your governance exercise is bringing it to life. There is no point in putting a great deal of effort into your governance activities if you haven't 'sold data governance' to the organisation. Since governance tends to have people running for the hills or looking for work-arounds before they even know the context, then you need to convey the importance, applicability and benefits of data governance and the approach you are taking. Hence, why over-governing is not a great starting point. What is your simple and easy-to-understand elevator pitch when it comes to data governance, and how can you convey that message broadly?

How do you get people involved and bring them on the journey with you? There is more about this in Chapter 19 on the data revolution, but make sure that you understand the different ways of bringing people with you, actively engage with them in a meaningful way (one-page instructions left on people's desks does not count as active engagement if it's all you are doing and has never worked before). Think about mapping your stakeholders and trying to understand them before looking at ways of helping them to understand and 'get' data governance.

We'd even suggest that by just putting some basics in place and then growing them to the right level you are starting your journey on the right path, whereas if you over-govern, you will struggle to gain a reasonable level of compliance if you aren't directly involved.

The role of assurance

We know this is a bit of a leading question, but do you think that once you have created a lovely, neat garden you can then sit back through the whole summer and expect everything to stay in place just as you left it? Or do you nurture it and tend it to help it? Your data landscape is no different. Surely it's better to proactively monitor and slowly adjust than go after crisis after crisis. Data governance is not a one-time project, it is a continuous, iterative process that organisations should implement a step at a time and then constantly, iteratively improve. In fact the organisations that have most successfully introduced data governance did so by implementing their programme incrementally.

We have all seen businesses that celebrate those heroes who stand up in a crisis and guide the ship towards calmer waters. While solving something that is catastrophic can make you feel like a hero, it really isn't a great way to run a business, lurching from one crisis to another. It's much better to manage your business so that you are steering in calmer waters and taking advantage of the tides pushing you the way you want to go. Use assurance as a way of having a level of comfort that you are in the calmer waters.

The maturity model which we covered in Chapter 5 is a great way of benchmarking where you are and the differences you are making. Performing a maturity model assessment on a regular basis demonstrates the progress you are making (hopefully) and highlights the areas that you really should focus on next. When you are coming up with how you want your assurance to work, remember to have different levels of assurance activities rather than a one-size-fits-all approach. We list some ideas here:

- **self-assurance** – this can be light-touch, from the centre or locally controlled governance; normally a questionnaire style that is completed locally and used to decide if you need to undertake further assessment
- **light central** – basically of the same as your first maturity model assessment but based area by area; you can employ comparisons here and hence an element of competition – healthy competition
- **in-depth assessments** for where you know you have a problem area.

I would advise that a data owner in any organisation puts a robust data governance structure in place from which everything else can flow. This will help to drive commercial value and ensure that the organisation is fully compliant.

(Nina Barakzai, Head of Data Protection and Privacy, Sky Group)

19
The data revolution

Introduction

This chapter suggests that while change is inevitable it can be managed. How we can help to get the best from the changes is explored and a model to help with creating lasting engagement is proposed.

Sustainable change

Lots of words have been written on paper about the data revolution and the impact that it will have on society, with predictions ranging from 'the sky is falling' to 'AI will lead to scenes from the film *Wall-E* becoming our new reality (where we become so used to having everything done for us that we lose the ability to do anything for ourselves)'. We tend to think about that being the external data revolution, i.e. what is happening outside our organisations, and we're not sure that we have a great deal to add on this one, other than that, with every other social revolution on record, while it was a bit of a rollercoaster ride as you went through it, what came out at the other end meant more jobs - albeit jobs that hadn't even been thought of before it happened. However, the world we live in is constantly evolving - we obviously don't remember our careers advisors at school telling us we could be a Chief Data Officer someday if we worked really hard - so that is part of the rich tapestry of life.

Though that may be what is seen as the external data revolution, what we want to focus on is the internal one. While talking about an internal data revolution may seem odd, it makes perfect sense when you think about it. As CDO, you have been brought in to convince the company that it has an asset that it has not yet valued and it now needs to modify its behaviour in order to look after it appropriately.

The most important thing to remember is that change is about people. Too often we get caught up in making a technical change work, making sure people know about using the practical aspects of the technology, or the way it looks from the outside. Too many organisations are doing a wonderful swan dance - looking calm, serene and totally in control while under the surface everyone is paddling for all they are worth. Real change is about people, and this is where everything we talk about regarding hearts and minds comes into play. Helping people understand why you want them to change their behaviour and convincing them of it creates sustainable change; anything less will result in slide back into what they believe is BAU.

The first thing should be so blindingly obvious that it's often overlooked, but please make sure you know what you want the change to look like. What is the outcome that you are hoping to achieve and how will you know when you get there? Do you even know exactly where you want to be, or do you just know the direction of travel that you want to go in, with an interim target? Either will work, as long as you are being honest with yourself and the organisation.

In the most simple terms it's about setting your direction and then executing it well. Simple - right? Well, as simple as that sounds it can be a little bit more difficult to make change stick. Sustainable change is something that people embrace and you can continue to build on.

Resistance to change

You will be imposing a culture change, and some people within your organisation will feel as if it has been forced upon them. However, if you do it right you can pull off a bloodless regime change, with everyone converted. Change is hard for people – we have great swathes of examples where people will dig themselves into a hole and not move, even when they can see the futility of their actions. If you address a whole group of people and ask them who wants to see change happen you will have a sea of hands, demonstrating what a great idea they think it is. Now ask the same group who wants to change, and you won't see quite as enthusiastic a response. It really is human nature to resist change and assume that a more established process is better: as studies have proved, people have a very reliable and tangible preference for things that have been around longer. For instance, people would have more favourable attitudes to things like acupuncture if they had been told it had been around for over 2,000 years than if they believed it had been around for 200 years. There is something in us that equates how long something has been in use with how good it is. This is a rational approach and has probably saved lives somewhere down the millennia. If a way of working has stood the test of time, then it is probably superior in some regards. So, it isn't just that people fear change, which we also think is a factor, but that they have a voice in their heads telling them that if they have been doing something for a long time, then that way is better.

However, this isn't the most accurate indicator of how good something is for our companies; it has in fact led to inertia and resistance to change. It is an unconscious bias that the vast majority of us hold, and you need to understand this, and how uncomfortable you are going to make the individuals within the company, before you will make things better. Just walking in and assuming that what you are selling is such a no-brainer that they would have to be stupid not to jump on the bandwagon isn't going to help you win friends and influence people.

The other factor that you should also be aware of is how many times people feel they have been around this before. Have there been other change programmes that announced they were concerned with data; have you got the change fatigue to deal with on top of everything else? Forewarned is forearmed. You will be faced with additional challenges if you are an FCDO Replayed, and if Gartner were right in their prediction there will now be a growing number of these.

Overcoming resistance

Take time to understand what position people are coming from, what is the status quo and what they are fighting to preserve. It will help you to articulate the whys behind what you are doing. Motivation is key to making any kind of change happen. Another wonderful thing about humans is that once we understand why we are being asked to do something different we are more prepared to look objectively at the change.

For example, we worked with a company that wanted its front-line staff to complete another four questions on a form that they had already filled in on a computer. The company couldn't understand the data from the form because over 98% of responses were exactly the same, when it was expecting variations in the data. It wasn't hard to surmise that the responses they were getting were directly related to where the answer was in the drop-box that came up for those questions – in other words, when the list came up the top item was clicked, so there was no accuracy in the answers. The front-line staff had been given no information other than 'The form has been updated and can you please complete these extra questions?' Not exactly excessive training. The problem in this case was a simple one, but very indicative of the way to tackle a lot of these problems. Following conversations with some of the staff to understand what was happening and why, a really brief e-mail was sent to everyone telling them why the information was needed, what it was being used for and how it would benefit them. The overnight difference in the responses was amazing; the company now had a set of data it could use.

This area is covered briefly in Chapter 5, but here we are giving you a bit more detail about why you are doing some of those things such as creating a vision and focusing on engaging with people. Someone has to lead the change – that would be you! No change happens completely spontaneously, someone somewhere started it. When it comes to the data revolution you need to be the one out front; don't be frightened to share the limelight, get more sponsorship. If the whole of your management team are committed and are prepared to demonstrate their commitment you will be visibly telling people that there is a new way of working in place and that it isn't going away. Words aren't enough here, everyone has to lead by example; to repeat an old cliché, 'Be the change you want to see'. There doesn't have to be just one leader, share the load. Why should you do all the work when you don't have to? Just make sure you are all heading in the same direction, otherwise it will be really confusing for the company and could easily do more harm than good.

Be clear about what you want to happen by creating your vision and then creating a strategy to execute that vision. This underpins your data nirvana, gives you the basis of the compelling story that you are selling to the company to convince them to come on this exciting journey with you, and develops the clarity that you need to keep everyone focused on the same goal. You know what 'good' looks like, so use that, be evangelical about this picture of the future that you are painting. Remember to also create a sense of urgency ('Why change now, can't it wait for a bit?' 'There is always something more pressing, so let's put this to the back of the drawer'). Use both a risk-based and a value-based approach here, blending the two to focus on the area that means the most to your company; identify the threats and demonstrate the value you have to gain. Do your research, find competitors in the same vertical sector who have achieved some success in parts of your vision already. Find trusted partners who have done a similar thing with successful outcomes. Add a range of voices and stories to your message. It might not be the whole vision, but it may be an example of data governance, or data tooling or data capability. Quite simply put, 'if you respect them and they are succeeding why not take a look at what they are doing?'

Communicating the vision

There is no point in doing any of this work if you don't tell anyone about it – so how do you do that? This is where the engagement comes in. We wish we had a pound for every time we have seen an organisation try to elicit a change by sending out mass e-mail communications and wondering why people aren't doing what they are told. We all know that this isn't the best method for making change happen, but because it is so quick and easy it seems to be the default position. The method that we have always preferred is using advocates: people listen to people they know and trust, and they are more likely to modify their behaviour if someone they respect gives them a good reason to do so. No matter how good you are at relationship building, unless the whole company is less than ten people you won't know everyone in it, hence the advocates. An advocate is someone who shares your vision, believes in the future you are creating and wants to work towards that future. Advocates don't always start off by being quite so passionate; on many occasions we have worked with advocates who have been 'volunteered'. While it would be nice to have committed, passionate supporters from day one, you are more likely to have sceptics who prefer the current mode of operation. By being clear, concise and committed to your vision, listening to their concerns and addressing them while promoting the positives, you can turn these sceptics into your biggest supporters.

As CDOs we've called our advocates the information champions, and we talk about their role in Chapter 10. We have used the multi-hub and spoke model (Figure 19.1) to really good effect.

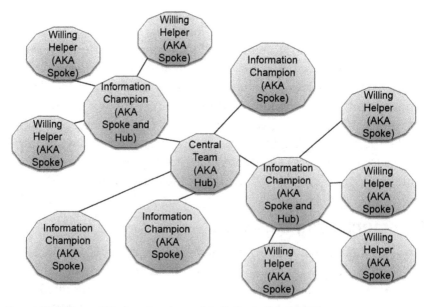

Figure 19.1 *The multi-hub and spoke model of information champions*

Picture your central team as the centre of excellence who carry a burning light of good practice when it comes to nurturing your information. You pass the torch to each of the information champions so that they have their own light while you keep the central flame burning. You encourage them to share the light around each of their own areas, so you slowly spread your message across the whole organisation in quite an organic way that will feel more natural and less abrasive.

This is just one example and assumes a central hub, but the diagram in Figure 19.1 could take many forms; you could have many centres of excellence with some form of uniting mechanism, or a very centralised team. Don't put in place a model that doesn't fit with how the organisation likes to work. You can stretch the boundaries, but cannot put in place an alien concept.

This also works with networked data teams; for example, including your data protection team, information security and/or your analytics teams in the model would provide clarity on how everyone works together. They don't have to work in the same line management to be able to work together well, as long as you take the time to clearly articulate (and agree!) who is responsible for what, where the grey areas are and what you are going to do when you come across them. Build those good relationships and structures so as to be able to leverage all the different skills you have.

Identify all of your stakeholder group. There are different groups within your organisation and if you try to use the same tactics with each one, then it may land well with some and annoy others. Understanding your different groups and their different motivations will help you to tailor your messages and ways of engaging with them for maximum impact.

Don't assume that everyone learns or communicates in the same way; everyone absorbs information differently. Also, each stakeholder group will be impacted upon differently; have you understood the impact on each one, and what that really means for them. While you need to be clear, consistent and tenacious about your vision, you need to constantly modify how you deliver that to the information champions in order to get the best from them. Listen to the cues they give you about what makes sense to them, and work with those. Use e-mail if that helps, but don't make it your be all and end all; try everything in your repertoire and see what works best, then do more of that. Once you start putting your message out, have a constant process of refinement and redeployment going on, and then repeat.

Remove the obstacles to help the information champions on their journey, whether those obstacles are poor tools or processes, training gaps or generally incorrect perceptions. Find out what is stopping them or making their life difficult and deal with it. Make the new path easier than returning to the old one (use the shared pain: it can be a great bonding exercise). While we will never cease to be amazed by the resourcefulness and creativity of human beings in keeping the status quo in place, when constantly presented with an easier journey they do start to follow the path of least resistance. Make sure that you take time to celebrate those successes - positively reinforce the right behaviour!

When you are building your change programme don't fall into the trap functions. It can seem easy to build it around the silos or different departments, but remembering that data doesn't sit in silos means that you should take an opportunity to break these down where you can.

A key area to look at is how skilled your organisation is around data literacy. We don't expect everyone to know Python and be fully conversant in analytics, but it really does help if everyone is pulling in the same direction.

Let's start with the basics - what is data literacy? We have seen lots of different definitions of data literacy, but the one that we think is the best is the ability to read, analyse, work with and argue with data. We think it should also be extended to include the creation of data as well as understanding that arguing with data has two meanings: can you use data to argue your point well, but can you also look at the data and interrogate it to ensure it is accurate?

In organisations with low levels of data literacy or awareness it is common to encounter duplication of data in local stores for offline manipulations; data quality issues are introduced because people don't understand the potential of the data; and often behaviours are driven by the fear of consequences rather than by a deep understanding of the value of data. Data literacy is important because it helps everyone to make the most out of the company data. It helps in making sure your data is as accurate as possible when it comes into your organisation, through streamlining tasks and with everyone making decisions. Data can be important or not, but you have to be data literate to understand the difference. As everyone becomes more aware of data and how to treat it, the chances of a data breach will be reduced and the possibility that a spark of innovation will be found will increase. As organisations become more data literate they are more likely to share data, ask questions and become more evidence based in their decision making. Data literacy also extends to understanding across the business about how to get the best out of your 'investment in data'. Many change programmes have projects working in silos to achieve individual business outcomes, often based on technology change or upgrades. However, a data-literate organisation will be able to understand that across these projects and initiatives there will be a 'commonality' of data, a matrix of data, and this needs to be joined up to leverage the most from the investment. A truly data-literate organisation will be able to have that conversation across the executive, change teams, IT and data.

It's also clear to us that different levels of data literacy are needed for different job roles and areas in the organisation, because everyone will need different skills and levels of understanding depending on what their primary focus is.

Imagine a line that looks like the one in Figure 19.2.

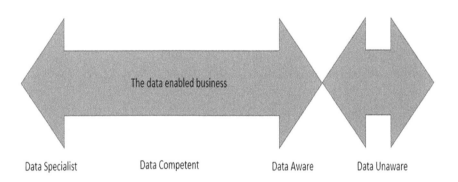

Data Specialist   Data Competent   Data Aware   Data Unaware

Figure 19.2 *Data literacy spectrum*

On the spectrum of data literacy there are obviously many gradings between the data aware and the data specialist, but the following are the basics.

Off the line really, but there is a category of the data unaware which can really impact on the development of a data-curious organisation.

To be data aware means that you can complete a form properly and accurately because you understand why you should and the possible impact it can have. This is where your basics are in place and everyone, at all levels, should be at least on this point on the scale.

To be a data generalist means that you can use reports and information to make decisions and can see the possibilities with the data you are and could be using.

The specialists are the more traditional roles that we assume are the data team, from the governance specialist to the data scientist. These are the people who really understand the art of data.

One thing we commonly see is that a strong data team, with low levels of data literacy across the rest of the organisation, means that accountability is deferred to the 'expert', who becomes a bottleneck answering a multitude of questions which could be answered elsewhere. They often come disillusioned with what they are doing because what they want to be focused on is the deep data questions which could enable a revolution for the organisation.

Now take a step back and in very general terms think about the different types of organisational roles, which tend to range from operational through tactical to strategic. How you use data at each level that (should) become more in tune with the nature of the role. At an operational level, data is used as an asset; normally it's generated at this level and used for simple reporting and tolerance metrics. Moving on to the more tactical roles, where you are making decisions with data to modify what you are working on, you are starting to ask some interesting questions. You then get to the strategic roles, where you should be leveraging the true insight you can get from data. By applying these two lines in a matrix you can start to break down different areas of your business into where they are and where they need to be (Figure 19.3 opposite).

You can see by using the matrix that a data literacy problem in any area can cause problems. For instance, with a highly literate operational workforce you should end up with a good quality of data to use, but if your tactical level cannot use it to make decisions, then they are wasting their time or, even worse, causing problems for the strategic level. For instance, picture a large infrastructure programme which has a great

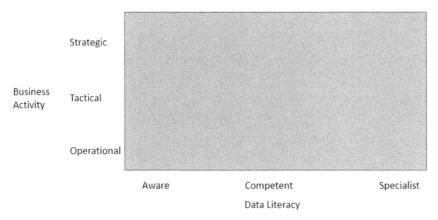

Figure 19.3 *Data literacy spectrum and business activity matrix*

project manager who knows problems are occurring and is reporting them accurately; however, their manager, who should be using that report to decide where to move support or to raise points of concern, 'tweaks it' to make it look more palatable because they don't understand why they shouldn't do that. This normally leads to a strategic level who happily plough on, unaware that they are sitting on an overspend ticking time bomb. At the other end of the spectrum you have strategic levels in organisations that have poor data literacy skills and refuse to acknowledge what the data is telling them - think Kodak and the digital camera.

By using this matrix you can start to group where different areas of the business are and where you want them to be. Then you can put plans into action which directly relate to moving each area on in a way that resonates with them. It's also useful to think about the different stages they would go through, and if you need them to. For example, would you want your call centre staff to have the same level of data literacy as your head of analytics, or do they have a different skill set and just need to have a good level of awareness?

You can have different tools in your tool bag and apply the same tool to a number of different groups, but still make it appear personalised to them.

A simplification of this is shown in Figure 19.4 on the next page.

Note that not everything in your tool bag would necessarily be termed education, some of it is engagement, and then we start talking

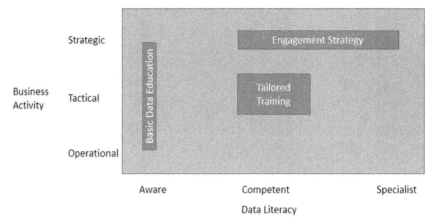

Figure 19.4 *Data literacy spectrum and business activity with examples*

about the hearts and minds battle that we have spoken about in earlier chapters. This is really the time to kick that into high gear; people who understand why they need to learn something different and change their behaviours are much, much more open to learning a new skill or way of working.

All of this feeds into your engagement and change management activities around your projects or transformations.

Be careful of your metrics when it comes to making a change. You will measure something, whether it is key performance indicators or early warning indicators; just remember that what you measure drives behaviours. We had a helpdesk reporting to us; we had reasonable customer care scores but nothing startling. One of the key measures driving the team's performance was how quickly they could close the first-line call. So naturally the first line weren't really trying to help the customer, they were targeted at passing it on as fast as possible, which created a load on the second line and didn't exactly make the customers happy either. After getting rid of that measure of how many calls first line could close on the first phone call, the customer care scores went through the roof. The first-line advisors trained themselves in some of the calls they would have happily passed over under the old regime; they were happier, as they enjoyed the variety of their role more, the customers were happy because over 80% of the calls were now resolved within one phone call (which might go on for 30 minutes, but that was preferable to the possible three-day wait to get the second-line team to solve the problem) and it had a knock-on effect on the second-line support and beyond, who all had more time to deal with the more interesting problems. It saved money, as less was being sent out to our suppliers to solve for us because we just didn't have the time to focus on them. It was a true win-win all round, achieved by thinking carefully about how we measured what we were doing.

The measures should be part of your assurance activities; even a Maserati needs a tune-up now and then, just to make sure it is running optimally. As with all the processes you have put in place, weed the path, check the signposts are still in place and are clear and make sure that everyone still buys in to the journey.

Lastly, don't expect any kind of meaningful culture change to take place overnight; you are looking at a journey you can measure in years, not months, so to keep the interest up you are going to have to demonstrate that the path is the right one and that it's worth staying the course. Here you can use your quick wins (discussed in Chapter 5). Nothing makes people sit up and take notice more than when you actually demonstrate a positive outcome. It makes them think that if you could achieve that in the short term, then they could buy in to the possibility of what they can achieve in the long term, building on these successes. Just don't rest on your laurels. Take time to celebrate those successes, promoting the 'art of the possible', demonstrate that the path to data nirvana is littered with great outcomes and benefits. Build your programme with a sustainable change in mind.

While you are celebrating your successes, just check that they are the successes you wanted to achieve. Have you completed your journey or at least headed in the right direction, or has the impact not been quite what you intended? Check your alignment and try to adjust mid-flight if you can.

We are writing this following the onset of the COVID-19 pandemic, so we think it's important to address this point. It's fair to say that it is one of the biggest global crises in modern history, having impacts that we will see the ramifications of for a long time. Anyone who tells you that lockdown wasn't tough would be lying, but that doesn't mean that we can't also treat what we experienced as an opportunity to learn. The data lessons that we can learn from a crisis help us to better prepare for the next inevitable challenge, and will ensure that we're able to better navigate ourselves through them in the future, all of which relates to the internal data revolution.

It's important to remember that crises have a tendency to blindside you. We believe that data is fundamental to navigating a path through whatever the world throws at us; we also need to realise that there aren't many situations where we'll have all the data at hand, ready to inform our decisions.

We don't live in an ideal world where perfect data is readily available and abundant, so the most important lesson that a crisis can teach us about data is that we should be ready to adapt and use what we can while managing the inevitable gaps in our understanding. Not having all of the data in front of you is not an excuse for refusing to make a decision (and doing nothing is making a decision, albeit often the wrong one!).

With the COVID-19 crisis, like so many other smaller crises, we have had to adapt quickly. What we have to acknowledge is that by using imperfect data and adapting to make a decision without all the necessary information the chances are that we'll make a bad call at some point. The second lesson, though, is that we have to learn to be okay with making mistakes, as long as we are quick to pick ourselves up and try again. When it comes to data-driven decision making, you have to predict, test and then re-predict. If you were right the first time – great! If not, learn from your first attempt, try something new and test again.

The other key lesson in how best to utilise data, especially with regard to a crisis, is to work collaboratively. Sharing data is one of the most important things we can do to strengthen our own decision-making processes. We can improve the quality of our data by acknowledging that someone else might have information that could be useful for us. Countries across the world experienced peaks of COVID-19 at different times, and we have been able to learn from those with earlier peaks, advancing our medical understanding of the virus and informing public policy decisions by learning from their experiences. Working collaboratively helps to build a fuller data set, which inevitably leads to fewer mistakes and more informed decision making.

When all is said and done, the COVID-19 crisis is first and foremost a tragedy. If we're able to learn lessons from our experience of it, though, by acknowledging that our data will never be perfect, our need to adapt quickly and the benefits of working collaboratively, then we will be better prepared to navigate through the next crisis that the world or our organisation throws at us.

20
Advice to business owners, CEOs and the board

Introduction

This chapter examines why the CEO might need advice about a CDO and provides seven pieces of advice about that relationship. It also looks at how to recruit a CDO, which could be extended to include other senior data roles, and some good advice is provided by front-line recruitment professionals.

Does the business need a CDO?

This is an easy question to answer if you are having problems with data or there are massive opportunities that require a strong focus on data, but maybe not as easy to articulate in other circumstances. Just like as you originally start a business you tend to be doing all the roles and bring in other people as you can to support you when the time is right – i.e. they pick up an area that you know you need help with or you don't have the right skills to fully capitalise on – you can think about it that way in your organisation.

So, do you have a highly literate data workforce, senior leaders who are really owning data and no problems? If so, then maybe you don't need to think about a CDO just yet. If your business relies on a great deal of data and is struggling with the complexity of what it is facing, then you need to jump on the bandwagon.

Let's be honest, it is simply not realistic to say that every organisation must have a CDO in order to work. If you are a small charity with 40 people working for you, we wouldn't advocate for a CDO to be one of those 40 (a competent data person, yes, but not a CDO). If you are a multinational company who knows its competitors are doing things faster, more easily and more innovatively, then absolutely yes. And let's face it, the title (CDO) may be a challenge for some organisations. What they may need, and call it what you will, is a data leader, someone to be accountable and responsible for the leverage of value and insight from data.

We can't tell you definitively if you need a CDO or not, but we can help you to think about the factors that make one useful or even essential.

- Do you operate with a great deal of data?
- Is there a high degree of duplication and rework?
- Do you trust your data?
- Is innovation stifled because you can't share information?
- Are other companies moving into your traditional space who don't have the wealth of knowledge that you do about your customer base, but who are winning market share?

After the decision has been made

Some pieces of advice can be given to the business owner about the CDO after the decision has been made to recruit one:

1 Every business owner should devote some time to thinking about data and discussing data in their business. A CEO spends time

every day, week, month, quarter or year thinking about other assets such as human resources, finance, physical assets, facilities and customers, and in each of these cases they have very senior colleagues, probably in the C-Suite, who look after these assets for them. So perhaps a wise CEO would give some time to thinking about data, especially if there is a desire to become a data-enabled business or if the importance of data is beginning to be understood. Perhaps data should be a standard agenda item for the leadership team. The businesses which are looking after their data are the businesses with an advantage and with efficiencies. Innovation and opportunities sit within the data; most discussions about disruption in any sector will involve a discussion about data.

2   The CEO should understand where and how data is used within the business and who is using the data. The CEO may not appreciate how important data is to customer services, or how it could transform customer services if used properly. The CEO may not see the opportunities in business efficiency through asset management driven via data. It is the CDO whose role it is to focus on this and to highlight the best (and worst bits) to senior stakeholders.

3   If the CEO perceives that data does or will play an important role in the future of the business, they should recruit a CDO. There is a danger that 'data' roles get delegated to a too-junior role or to the wrong team. Data is a specialist skill and is not synonymous with IT or with any department that is a heavy user of data. Just because they use it doesn't mean they know how to look after it. A good driver isn't necessarily a good mechanic. Often, data initiatives or transformations fail because the job is vested in a role that is too junior in the organisation's hierarchy and the role doesn't have the authority, credibility or cross-business scope to develop and communicate the vision or build the necessary relationships. It is inevitable that someone in a junior role will take a tactical approach because they don't have the opportunity, mandate or experience to be strategic. If a CDO is needed, make the decision, move quickly and empower them.

4   Think carefully about where to put your CDO. Ensure that they are sitting in the correct directorate or line of business and that

they are reporting to the right person. This will of course depend on the nature of the business, on the existing data environment and the organisational structure. But here are two pieces of advice to help get this one right: if the CEO wants the CDO to be a driver of transformation and expects big things, first make sure that the CDO has some means of reporting directly or at least very closely to the CEO and the leadership team or board. The more bodies that are positioned between the CEO or board and the CDO, the more of the message, the passion and the expertise will be lost. Second, make sure that the person the CDO is reporting to 'gets' data.

5   Support your CDO and empower your CDO. If you have an FCDO, this is your first person in this role. They will be alone, trying to build something new, without an existing team, trying to communicate the vision and strategy. They will need support, and that support needs to be visible and felt by the CDO, but also visible to the business. If you don't support, or aren't seen to be supporting, your CDO, they will fail and probably leave your organisation. At that point you will find it increasingly difficult to get a replacement. However, if you've recruited the wrong type of CDO and/or got them in the wrong place, then face up to this sooner rather than later, and/or be prepared to hear this from them.

6   The CEO needs to appreciate, and play a role in, keeping the balance between risk and innovation. A CDO will approach risk in a way that is new to the organisation, often through innovative proof of value or an agile fail-fast methodology. The CEO will need to understand the approach of seeking and scaling: seeking and trying innovations and then scaling those that are of value into operation as quickly as possible. So, while the CEO should of course manage risk, he should understand that new delivery approaches and project methodologies are not necessarily more risky.

7   Stop throwing bodies at a problem and look for the smart solution. There is a legacy in business of 'work-arounds'. Often these involve the manual re-keying of data, or the manual manipulation of data in spreadsheets, or the manual building of reports. All of these processes draw in more and more bodies,

often cheaper offshore bodies. This is not only an ongoing overhead but a potential root cause of errors in data and the information produced. Tools are available to integrate, migrate, move, transform, integrate and report on data: these tools can automate the processes, providing greater efficiencies and accuracy. A CDO will be able to lead this transformation.

As Caroline and Peter state, the organisation needs to trust and have confidence in the CDO and so I think it will be telling to see whether the business gives the CDO the power and support required. A good gauge of the real intent to deliver on a data-driven strategy.

(Jeff Nott, Account Director, UK & Ireland Public Sector, Alfresco)

This ties in to the advice from Jez Clarke at Eden Smith, which specialises in working with business leaders to help them find the right data specialists:

This is a long-term investment, there may be some low-hanging fruit which the CDO will identify but overall this is a huge business transformation. My points of advice to any business owner before recruiting a CDO are:

1. Be very hard on yourself and ask the question 'What business problem/s are you trying to solve and WHY?' The CDO will want to know.
2. Are you fully 100% committed to seeing a DATA strategy through? While this business transformation could both save and make millions, it will take lots of time and huge commitment.
3. The CDO will require 100% support to make this happen, give them the full support required.
4. Ensure your business is prepared to invest in the technology and people required to drive the change – seek advice from experts before making a commitment.
5. Be innovative and open in your recruiting strategies – use specialists, not generalists.
6. Showcase your passion for embarking on a data strategy.
7. Engage the WHOLE business – delivering a data strategy will require the support of every employee, not just a select few.

8 Expect some resistance from certain areas in your business; be prepared to sell the concept with the help of the CDO.

9 Don't try to 'eat the elephant' – such large business transformation will require a 'go slow to speed up' approach for success.

10 Let the CDO do their job, look for small successes to start with, which with good internal case study will help drive a new, data-driven culture.

Be 100% committed to delivering a data strategy, allow your newly appointed CDO to do their job and give them your FULL support. Expect and plan for some internal resistance, go slow to speed up and invest well. This is an exciting journey of transformation, ensure ALL of your employees understand the value of their input.

How to recruit a CDO

This chapter and Chapter 14, 'How to present yourself as a CDO', have the same aim: to stop failure and ensure that the right business gets the right CDO and vice versa.

Gartner Inc. predicted in 2016 that 90% of large organisations would have a CDO role by 2019. Gartner went on to predict that 15% of CDOs would move on to CEO, COO, CMO or other C-level positions by 2020.

Once a business has taken a decision to recruit a CDO, how should they go about this?

Most organisations will need to use a recruiter or head-hunter, unless they have a very developed and experienced in-house team, and, even if they have, this is a really specialist role, so they might want a little advice. If the route of recruiter is chosen, the first step is the realisation that because the CDO is a specialised role, many recruiters may not have the skill, contacts or market knowledge to deliver what is required. This is still a relatively niche role to fill, so make sure you have the right support. The good agencies will know the market and know who and what is available and who can be approached.

Regardless of where the CDO role is placed, their biggest challenge is going to be being able to hold different conversations across a very broad range of stakeholders.

(Hany Choueiri, Chief Data Officer, Bank of England)

An early part of the process, as with any job, is to consider the role and where it will sit in the organisation and to write a job description or specification. Getting the line of reporting right is very important; if it is wrong this alone may deter good candidates from applying. Think carefully about the relationship with IT: does the CDO report to IT or does the CDO sit alongside IT? This is probably the biggest question to be answered in the line of reporting. How close will the new CDO be to the CEO and leadership team? Again, this will be a crucial factor for the good candidates. It would be wise to partner with a good recruiter and enlist their help in writing the job description, specification and package. The recruiter should understand and be able to advise on the market conditions: the sort of package that will attract the right candidates of the appropriate skill level and experience and how much lead time will be required to attract them, process the applicants and get a person in the role. It is worth bearing in mind that it isn't all about the package; there will be other factors that will be important to the good candidates:

- Location is an obvious factor.
- The line of reporting, as discussed above, is less obvious but will be important to the best candidates.
- The nature of your data: in simple terms, does your data provide 'interest' to the data geek? Are you in an interesting market or do you have an unusual breadth and type of data? A good candidate may rate the 'data' over the package. An opportunity to work with customer data and asset data may be attractive – or customer data and supply chain data, or financial data and regulatory data.
- The size of your problem: some people are really interested in the next problem to solve and get really excited by the bigger, wicked problems.
- Your existing data environment may be such a mess that you struggle to attract candidates, or it may be too mature and clean to attract candidates.
- The point above also requires you to think about which type of CDO you need. Take a look at Chapters 12 and 13.
- Your data aspirations as an organisation will be key. Are you interested in really following through on a transformation, or are you looking for a stable pair of hands?

It is very important that the recruiter and you articulate all of these in the marketplace and to potential candidates. Just to reiterate, it isn't all about your brand or the package. Good CDOs are in high demand and they can afford to pick and choose. The good recruiter who understands the role and the marketplace will validate your requirements and expectations. They will probably be able to undertake some confidential early market engagement and provide a guide as to who is available and what the initial feedback from the market may be. The value of the recruiter is that they may know individuals who are not actively seeking a position but who may be interested in your opportunity and offer.

The role is emerging and not yet fully established - Gartner estimates the number of CDOs and Chief Analytics Officers more than doubled in 2015 to 1,000 - up from 400 in 2014. Statistically significant numbers are hard to come by, but CDO salaries vary widely, depending on the organisation and sector, but good skills and experience are in short supply so it tends to be a hot market.

We do like to keep it as simple as possible, so we can summarise as follows:

- Think about whether the time is right for you to have a CDO and whether you will get the value you want from having one.
- Think about the type of CDO you need.
- Are you prepared to set them up to succeed?
- Are you ready for the journey or are you looking for a quick fix?

21
Conclusion

To say the world has moved on a bit since the first edition of this book would be an understatement; the world of data has moved even faster and continues to do so, and that rate of forward movement seems to be accelerating. The leaders are leading from a greater distance and others are falling behind. Data is becoming the differentiator. It is probably more nuanced than that. Where organisations have embedded data deeply into the heart of their change, transformation and business processes then that has become the true differentiator in the markets and verticals. We still hope that this book has done what it aimed to do, which was to share our knowledge and the knowledge of the countless data professionals we work with in order to help you. We have enjoyed and been privileged to beg and borrow knowledge from our fellow data professionals, who have been most generous with their time and ideas, and we both know we have added massively to our own experience and learning through this process. There were also times that we both wondered why we thought this would be a good idea again, but thankfully they were relatively few and far between! On the contrary, we have found this a rewarding and stimulating exercise. We've listened a lot over the past two years, and it has been interesting and encouraging to note that there are now more, and an increasing number, of well-informed voices to listen to.

This excerpt from the first edition is as true now as it was then – data is still an exciting place to be and we feel even more strongly how lucky we are.

> We strongly believe that data is the catalyst for innovation and transformation and that it will reshape the way that organisations are

structured and how they operate. A successful organisation will be one that collects the right data, stores it well, makes it accessible to the business and uses it to gain insight and wisdom, enabling it to make accurate and powerful decisions. Furthermore, we believe that organisations need a Chief Data Officer, a specialist data professional, to deliver this data capability to drive the innovations and transformations that the organisation requires.

'Data' is currently an exciting place to be. While there is a paradigm shift for organisations that are striving to become data-driven, or data-enabled, instead of the old ways of working and perceptions of what drives a business. We feel very lucky to be data professionals in this moment of 'industrial revolution'. We believe that the Fourth Industrial Revolution is presenting organisations and the data professional with a unique moment in time, we are at that pivot point. Now is pivotal for those organisations which are going to put data at the heart of their organisation and truly leverage its power. It is also pivotal for the data professional who should be stepping forward now at this moment and lead.

What we have seen over the past few years is a growing awareness of data that hasn't been driven just by new legislation, but by boundaries being pushed both positively and negatively, such as by new medical advances or some rather unethical uses of data coming to public attention. A fear of data bubbled up to the surface that still percolates; however, we are now seeing an understanding of the inherent value of data rising too, and we feel very strongly that this drive for value (balanced by the right ethics and governance) will overcome the majority of the fear to demonstrate how we use data as a force for good. It's such a cliché but we couldn't resist: it's not what you've got but how you use it that matters. This awareness has grown beyond the legislation which brought attention to, especially, personal data; it has grown as the data literacy of business leaders has grown. CEO and boards are asking better and more informed questions about data within their organisations: 'What is the risk that data poses for us? Why is our data so hard to use? How much do we spend on data? Could better use of data make us more efficient? What do we do with all this data? Who owns the data in our organisation?' Some of the business leaders are now even asking about 'low-code', DataOps and data maturity. This is a long way forward from where we were when we wrote the first edition of this book.

Security, sustainability and ethics around data have to become non-negotiables in order to overcome fear of data, along with education, engagement and higher levels of data literacy if we are really going to see the potential of data delivered.

Data is already playing a greater part in our lives, in some cases in ways that we don't look for and recognise. The level of automation that data delivers is prevalent in how autocorrect and autocomplete manage our text messages and documents for us. We're convinced that autocorrect is on a mission to drive us insane as, because of our fat fingers, it constantly corrects 'data' to 'dara' – but it will learn eventually. Moving on, this is only one small indication of how data will take the mundane tasks from us, allowing us the freedom to contemplate the wicked problems, the more challenging aspects of organisations that require an undefined spark of human imagination, maybe alongside the power of AI.

We can't assume, however, that everyone will want this, and that brings us to a key factor we which believe we all need to take into account going forward: choice. Choice is key to data and how we utilise it, now more than ever as people are becoming aware of how their data is being used. They want a choice in that, they want to have the choice of knowing what is happening to their data, which only comes through real transparency. They want to get to be able to choose how their data is being used and, we strongly believe, that they will pick services based on the way that organisations use their data, and how organisations talk about using their data (or not!). As data professionals we cannot ignore this. We talk about agile and how it aligned well with using data, but it's not just agile as a methodology but agile as a way of thought that we need to build in, regarding data. Our customers, our stakeholders have a choice and they will exercise that choice with data, so we have to be ready as businesses and organisations to be able to accept and, as responsible organisations, encourage that choice, pivoting our data-enabled business as necessary based on trusted data. You can do this only if you really understand your data within the organisation.

That all sounds exciting, maybe a little scary, but mostly exciting, and it just exemplifies why we think data is still pivotal to our businesses, organisations and even our societies. But will this really drive us to get the full value from data? We've seen organisations claim that they are becoming data enabled, but when you scratch below the surface it's a bit 'emperor's new clothes'. Please don't get us wrong, there are pockets of excellence that we have held up as exemplars of data's potential, but we still think we are scratching the surface of what data can do. We need to redefine what we think of as impossible and start to use our imaginations as a child would, without limitations, and then adapt to what they have around them. Think about the 'how', not the 'whether'. Then we may leverage the full potential that data offers, giving us the value that we all talk about. This can be frightening for many organisations; not so much for start-ups, many of whom start from this premise. But it can be frightening for organisations already in flight. This mindset is more than just 'innovation'; this mindset sits at the heart of an organisation and that is why we believe that organisations need a CDO, and this will become an increasing priority. If data, and how data is used, is going to be the differentiator, then surely organisations need someone to lead the change and maintain the focus on that while the wheels of the business continue to turn. To play this role highlights all that we discussed about the secret ingredients of the CDO, how to present yourself as a CDO, the team you build and relationship with the rest of the C-Suite.

This is a journey that we all share, either as data leaders or part of the data team, or as business leaders. Data is here, it's going to stay, it's not going away and the forward-looking organisation will utilise the power of data as a differentiator. The learning on this journey never stops because organisations want to push the boundaries of how they are using their data as new technologies emerge to help us push those boundaries, as thought leadership evolves and as the data literacy of organisations increases. Once more we thank you for coming on this journey with us. This whole area is only as good as you help us to make it. Welcome to the wonderful world of CDOdom. Enjoy and spread the joy, the potential and value of data!

Index